Golden Eagles

Throughout the years I worked on the photographs for this book I met many people
who knew much about golden eagles. Without their help and encouragement, I doubt whether
I would have found ways of getting close to these birds. In recognition, I would particularly like
to thank the RSPB, Scottish Natural Heritage, Roy Dennis, Mike Tomkies,
Fraser Donald, David & Hazel Whitaker & family.

First published in Great Britain in 1996 by
Colin Baxter Photography Ltd
Grantown-on-Spey
Moray, PH26 3NA
Scotland

ISBN 0-948661-55-0

Printed in Hong Kong

Golden Eagles

Laurie Campbell
&
Roy Dennis

Colin Baxter Photography Ltd, Grantown-on-Spey, Scotland

Contents

The Golden Eagle

The early morning mist rises from the river and the sun burns through to reveal clear blue skies. Scattered pines on the distant hillside catch the sunlight as they shake free of a swirling bank of fog. It is as though a primeval world is coming to life. A black speck circles out of the dark green trees, hardly visible through binoculars – and my heart misses a beat. Is it an eagle? The huge bird comes down the glen, its great wings beating ponderously, and in a moment it is close enough for me to appreciate fully its size and dexterity on the wing. He passes over and searches for thermals rising from the warm slopes of the glen. As he spirals effortlessly up into the blue skies and disappears over the mountain, I again marvel at the sheer beauty of golden eagles in the Highland landscape.

There is no mistaking one's first sighting of an eagle. It is a special occasion for any bird watcher.

Cairngorms. 27 April 1960. My very first sighting of a golden eagle! I hiked up through the forest and crossed the top of the corrie to look down to Stac na h-Iolaire. Found a golden eagle brooding on a nest high in the rock face. Only her very golden head and huge bill were showing over the edge of the big bulky heap of sticks. She slowly lifted herself off the eggs and left the nest, lumbering away on her huge wings towards the south. Dark brown plumage with a golden mantle and head and tops of her shoulders. Long, heavy wings with upturned primaries. Bright yellow legs. I left quickly so she could return to the eggs.

An old friend, now gone, had told me where to look for this eagle. Younger colleagues have received similar help from me but in general it is not wise to disclose the location of eyries, for they are vulnerable. Instead, I suggest good vantage points to people who have asked me for help in seeing their first eagle. Usually it is a place with a broad panorama where eagles often fly. Locations where immature eagles gather are good choices. Sit still, watch the horizons, choose good weather – mid morning is a good time of the day – and be prepared to spend several hours waiting.

Harris, Western Isles. 9 January 1974. Drove to West Loch Tarbert and scanned the sea with binoculars; saw black-throated and great northern divers, and eight curlews on the shore. Turned round and saw two adult eagles above the rocky mountain side, then another three further to the east. One of these flew towards Beesdale while the other two

The Cuillin of Skye.

displayed with a little rollercoasting flight. Mobbed by nine ravens, they drifted away to the north-east. Otter fishing in sea by roadside, caught a very small fish and ate it at the surface. Saw another five golden eagles in the afternoon!

The golden eagle is one of the world's thirty species of eagle and as well as occurring in Britain it is widespread in the northern hemisphere. It belongs to the genus Aquila, the true booted eagles. Members have legs that are not bare, as in other birds of prey, but are feathered down to the base of their toes. Golden eagles occur from the Atlantic coasts of Europe and North Africa across Europe and Asia to the Pacific Ocean and throughout North America. There are six different races, or subspecies, of golden eagle in the world, with slight geographical differences in size and colour. The full Latin name is *Aquila chrysaetos*.

Spain. April 1988. I am driving across a dry dusty plain, the grass is parched and the spring flowers are dotted across the grassland ahead of me. In places the farmers have harvested their corn and they are starting to feed their cattle with hay gathered during the winter. This is the dry dusty interior of Spain. I have just passed the remains of a big stone house crumbling at the roadside, and around it were a dozen lesser kestrels revisiting old nest sites in the remains of the building. Some bee-eaters were flying by and a very pale red kite was quartering over a dry gully. As it hunted across long waving yellow grasses it flushed a young golden eagle which rose up from eating its prey. The bird was about two years old; it was very bleached, the plumage paler than any eagle I had seen before.

Adult eagles are usually uniformly brown with slightly darker marked colouring on the back and wings. The beautiful golden feathers are found on the head and nape. On the wing, eagles appear massive and can be seen with the naked eye more than a kilometre (almost a mile) away. A fully grown adult eagle measures 76–91 centimetres (30–36 in) from the tips of the beak to tail. Females are larger with an average wingspan of 2.2 metres (7 ft 2 in) and a weight of 4.6 kilogrammes (10.25 lb). Males are smaller, with an average wingspan of 2 metres (6 ft 7 in) and a weight of 3.9 kilogrammes (8.5 lb).

The plumage is variable, so that individuals are readily distinguished. Youngsters are much darker than their parents. In some birds the whole top and back of the head is a rich golden yellow, with dark brown flecks in the centre of the feathers. The pale golden colour on some birds runs down on to the feathers of the nape and its sides, giving the birds a golden shawl, and some birds are very yellow along the front edge of the wing to the wrist.

The eagle's bill is large and powerful and deeply hooked for tearing up its prey; the outer part of the bill is blackish horn and the base ivory-coloured with a brilliant yellow gape and cere (the fleshy part above the bill). Above the eye is a yellowy-green ridge, giving the bird a fierce look and shielding the pale tawny eyes of the adult. The feet are huge and yellow with long, black, sharp and powerful talons.

Taking flight and landing require much skill as the great wings are beat strongly and the tail is fanned for maximum control.

A frequently used weathered perch provides a good vantage point over hunting territory.

When they leave the nest, young birds have distinctive white panels in the centre of the wing at the base of the primary feathers and a white tail with a black band at the end. The white patches on the wings of the youngsters are very variable in extent and shape so that it is possible to tell individuals apart. One Swedish ornithologist, watching eagles at a food dump during the winter, identified over a hundred different individuals from their plumage characteristics. Once they reach the age of four, young birds start to acquire the darker adult plumage.

Eagles have a remarkable flying ability. They dive at high speed yet can quarter slowly, low across the ground and turn at a moment's notice to grab their prey in the long heather or among the rocks. They can swoop over the edge of corries and dive down after fleeing ptarmigan. The deadly power in their outstretched feet is awesome.

Morayshire. 24 October 1971. At noon went to Dava Moor, saw a kestrel on the big rock, then two golden eagles. The male was adult, the female two or three years old. The male displayed desultorily over the cliffs and then moved off to the west. The female dived about a hundred metres to strike at white hares in the heather, but missed, then she hunted along the east side of the road.

Mankind has had a long history of association with eagles, going back thousands of years. Early man painted them on cave walls. They were revered as gods in Babylon and Syria. In ancient Greece the golden eagle was the messenger of Zeus, ruler of the universe, who sometimes appeared as an eagle. A silver standard of a golden eagle with its wings extended was carried by Roman legions. In Israel eagles nested on Mount Sinai, symbolising Jehovah's protection. In more recent times, the golden eagle appears in the national emblems of Austria, Germany, Russia, Poland, France and Mexico.

In Scotland, Highland chieftains wear eagle flight feathers in their head dress and the eagle motif appears on eighteen of the historic arms of the Scottish clan chiefs. I remember a particularly poignant moment when my wife placed a golden eagle's feather on top of her father's coffin as he was laid to rest at the ancient burial ground of Cille Choirill in Brae Lochaber, Inverness-shire. Her father was a direct descendant of the chiefs of Clan MacDonell of Keppoch, and the laying of the eagle feather was a clan tradition.

In some countries, personal contact with live eagles flourished. In North America, one of the ultimate skills possessed by the Native Americans was to capture free-flying golden eagles by hand. A man was concealed in a camouflaged pit beside bait. When an eagle landed its feet were grabbed by the hidden brave. Ceremonial feathers were taken and the bird was released back into the wild. In this way, the captor gained the spirit of the eagle. To him the eagle was the Thunderbird, the creator of the world, the messenger of the gods, even the Great Spirit itself. In China and Mongolia, the ancient art of falconry dates back 4000 years. There, golden eagles were trained to hunt wolves and foxes.

A regurgitated eagle pellet contains undigested fur, feather and bone. These are often used for studies on eagle diet.

Hovd, Mongolia. 9 September 1990. Walked out of the dusty town past ancient earth walls. Brown shrikes on fences, yellow-browed warblers in the trees and about forty black kites overhead. Mongolian yurts (tents) with red and blue doors pitched on the edge of a grassy plain below the hills. Horsemen passing by with sheep and goats. A young boy showed us his father's trained eagle (bergut in his language). It was perched on a wooden block in a small shed beside their yurt, a brown leather hood over its head. It was used for hunting red foxes in winter. Later met a Kazakh who hunted with eagles. An old man mounted on a brown horse, his long coat was blue-black and velvety, made from animal skins. He wore a Kazakh hat and a silver belt embedded with jewels. In winter he'd spent many days on horseback with his friends hunting wolves and foxes with eagles.

The historic and cultural significance of eagles has not saved them from persecution in recent centuries. The most awful onslaught on eagles in Scotland took place in the last century. The Victorian slaughter of predators, including golden eagles, at the time of the popular craze for Highland sporting estates was incredible. The record books detail massive persecution of raptors. At Glengarry, Lord Ward engaged numerous gamekeepers and awarded bounties of £3–5 per bird or mammal killed. The keepers pursued the slaughter with undeviating rigour and attention, and the result was the destruction of about 4000 head of vermin in three years. This was done in the interests of increasing game for sport shooting. Similar activities were taking place elsewhere: the record books for two estates in Caithness list a total of 296 eagles destroyed between 1819 and 1826.

This persecution caused a large decrease in numbers of eagles, a decrease exacerbated by the taking of eggs for collections and skins for taxidermy. Throughout this century the persecution of eagles has continued despite increasing levels of protection, new wildlife legislation and widespread publicity and education. But in the last twenty years the situation has improved and numbers of eagles have increased. Nevertheless, a minority still illegally take eagles or their eggs from the wild. The Royal Society for the Protection of Birds (RSPB) has been necessarily active, endeavouring to strengthen protection for eagles.

Scottish Highlands. In April 1980 my RSPB colleague, David Pierce, visited an eagle territory near Laggan Bridge in Inverness-shire and found a female eagle incubating on one of the nests. He returned on 30 May and there was a young eaglet in the nest, which he estimated to be four weeks old. The site was visited again on 11 June when an adult flew off (and the chick was alive and well). But on 27 June the nest was empty and the chick had gone.

On 4 July the police from Kingussie interviewed the old shepherd, who was seventy-two years old and born in the glen. He was voluble and went on about eagles. He claimed great knowledge of the birds and said they were a nuisance for killing lambs.

The pointed feathers of the nape are very beautiful.

He claimed that two chicks had been blown out of a nest and he had given one to a falconer, who was searching for an eaglet.

The eaglet was removed from the falconer and sent back to Scotland. On 9 July, with the permission of the landowner, Roger Broad and David Pierce put the eagle back in its nest along with a plentiful supply of food. The young eagle stood up on its eyrie and flapped its wings. Almost immediately one of its parents appeared on the opposite hillside.

On the following day the youngster stayed on the eyrie, but the day after it flew from the nest and landed some 14 metres (45 ft) away. Subsequently, it called and flew with its parents. This was the first known case of a young eagle being successfully returned to a nest; remarkable given its enforced absence of eighteen days.

Once widespread in the British Isles, eagles are now virtually confined to the mountainous areas of Scotland, with only one or two pairs nesting in northern England. In many other countries, persecution and habitat loss have caused a decline, especially during the last century. Nowadays, eagles are closely associated with areas having low human populations and where nesting sites are generally inaccessible to disturbance.

A recent review of the status of the golden eagle in Europe by Dr Jeff Watson of Scottish Natural Heritage suggests that about 5600 pairs breed in Europe. The largest number is in Spain (about 1200 pairs), with Norway, European Russia, Scotland and Sweden each holding over 300 pairs. Information on trends in numbers reveals that most populations larger than 200 pairs are stable, but a decrease is still occurring in some Baltic countries and in parts of south-east Europe.

The European population is grouped in five bio-geographic regions with eagles living in quite different habitat types. These regions are: the north-west mountains of Scotland and Scandinavia; the eastern Baltic lowlands stretching from Finland across into Russia and the Baltic states; the western Mediterranean mountains from Spain, southern France and into Italy; the alpine mountain population in the Pyrenees and the Alps; and the population in the Balkan mountains running down from Hungary into Greece, Crete and the edges of Turkey.

The principle of using bio-geographic zones for the conservation of big birds such as eagles is sound because each population is quite distinct. The Scottish population of golden eagles comprises 7.5 per cent of the European population as a whole, but is over 22 per cent of the north-west mountain population.

I have always been interested in the people who have worked with eagles in Scotland. When I first started to watch eagles in Strathspey I read books by Seton Gordon, who had watched the eagles there in the 1920s and wrote eloquently about this magnificent bird.

I still have in my photograph collection a lovely picture taken of Seton not long before he died, on the Isle of Skye. He is standing on a road close to where he lived in Duntulm, talking to my friend Andrew Currie. In the background the headlands stretch to the Minch and the Outer Isles; Seton is standing there, talking about

No wonder this bird is called the golden eagle. The golden brown head is pronounced in many individuals while this close-up view shows well the bright yellow gape and cere (fleshy area above the bill) as well as the powerful hooked bill.

eagles, wearing his blue bonnet with its chequered headband; his old telescope is hanging over his shoulder, his long fawn gabardine coat hiding his tattered blue kilt and green stockings. He is steadying himself with his hazel stick and is asking if a nest he once knew is still active.

He first started to watch eagles before it was a popular pastime. Before him was H.B. MacPherson of Balavil, who photographed golden eagles at Gaick, near Kingussie, at the turn of the century and wrote one of the first books about the bird. *The Home Life of the Golden Eagle* is illustrated with beautiful black and white photographs, some of the very first ever taken of eagles in the wild, and MacPherson's writing evokes the real magic of the bird as revealed below.

27 May 1909. For the first time in my life I was now alone with eagles in a hiding place commanding a view of the nest. The young eagle lay asleep, like a mere bunch of white down, in the huge structure. The wind moaned in strange, piercing gusts, which echoed and re-echoed from the rocks, and the burn roared furiously in spate below ... through my peep-hole I could see the mist rolling in endless wreaths along the opposite face, though as yet the nest itself was clear... At 1.30 p.m. a dark shadow flitted across the peep-hole, and peering cautiously out, I saw the giant bird.

After the Second World War, Pat Sandeman and George Waterston travelled throughout the Highlands encouraging landowners, keepers and stalkers to protect eagles. The RSPB ran a reward scheme whereby people who guarded 'their' eagles, and managed to get the young ones to fly, were rewarded with between £10 and £20. During these travels they learned of new eyries and formed lasting friendships with people involved with eagles. I was fortunate to benefit from their friendship and guidance.

At the same time, the first researchers were looking at the eagles in detail. Leslie Brown, for instance, born in Scotland, but who had spent most of his life in East Africa, returned to study the eagles of his homeland. Other eagle enthusiasts such as Adam Watson (still following his lifelong studies of eagles in Deeside), Jim Lockie and Derek Ratcliffe, then of the Nature Conservancy, researching the effects of insecticides on eagles in the western Highlands, and Charlie Palmer, naturalist and photographer of Glasgow University, all encouraged people to become interested in eagles.

The late Lea MacNally, a famous Highland stalker, used his intimate knowledge of half a dozen pairs of golden eagles around Fort Augustus to write *The Ways of an Eagle*. He then moved to work in Torridon, where he continued his lifelong interest in eagles. Mike Tomkies lived in Ardnamurchan for nearly ten years and wrote movingly about his relationship with the eagles which nested in the hills near his remote cottage.

Over the decades many people have helped with the monitoring and protection of eagles in the Highlands and Islands. Friends such as Roger Broad, Ken Crane, Colin Crooke, Pete Ellis, Mike Everett, Kate Nellist, Dave Pierce, Jeff Watson, Doug Weir and many others fell under the spell of the golden eagle. All our lives have been enriched, not just by the eagles, but by our contact with the nature of wild places.

*An adult eagle checking
out the neighbourhood.*

Life
✦ in
Winter

New Year's Day in the Scottish Highlands and below me the great dark pine trees of the Caledonian Forest are dotted across the bare brown moors, stretching away to the south into the foothills of the Cairngorms. This is the home of my nearest pair of eagles. We are here to see our first eagle of 1992.

After the night-long festivities of Hogmanay and the seeing-in of the New Year few people are about! Some years I set myself the challenge of identifying the most possible species in one of the shortest days of the year. Once, I recorded one hundred in the Highlands on the first day of January, though it was a desperate struggle to get the last one, a barn owl, well after dark. Today, we set a modest target of fifty species in Strathspey.

Today's sighting of an eagle, though, was one of those superb occasions which will remain in my memory for ever. We'd been standing by the Land Rover for ten minutes looking towards the straggling pines in the strath below. A herd of seven red deer sauntered through the leggy heather looking for food, otherwise no wildlife stirred. There was no sign of our local eagles and their favourite roosts were empty.

1 January 1992. I suddenly looked up into the sky. It was as though I sensed the bird was there before I actually saw it. And there, well over 300 metres (1000 ft) above us, was a black speck of an eagle, already in full descent. Her wings were tucked in and she was stooping fast, hurtling towards the ground. Undoubtedly she could see her quarry somewhere on the ground ahead of me. Through my binoculars I followed her headlong dash straight into a few pine trees on the edge of the forest. Suddenly her wings were outstretched, her instantly spread tail checked her dive, and her talons shot forward as she thumped into the heather at the base of a huge Scots pine.

At the same moment, whirring wings exploded out of the heather and a female black grouse, a greyhen, hurtled away. The eagle struggled up from the ground, wings desperately flapping as she quickly resumed her pursuit. But by this time the greyhen had made her escape, twisting and turning low over the ground, through the pines. Her underwings flashed white as her brown and grey body strained to put as much distance as possible between her and her pursuer.

The eagle circled above the trees intently searching for her missed prey. She hovered briefly over a tree where she thought the bird had landed and then

Feeding on carrion in winter.

The snow-clad mountains of Glen Shee, winter home to the eagles.

side-slipped down among the branches. Five minutes later she spiralled up out of the woods. I could sense her disappointment. Her flight had no spring to it, and she drifted gently away towards the east, with a slow glide, slipping down into a clump of twenty ancient Caledonian pine trees.

Today she went hungry but there would be other days for hunting. Her mate is probably hidden in the trees, roosting quietly on one of the great limbs. She might have missed his help, because catching forest grouse is easier when a pair of birds hunts together in winter.

Black grouse and capercaillie are quite common in this area, with the black grouse preferring the open ground on the edge of the forest and the capercaillie keeping to the denser pine woodlands. Both are favoured prey for eagles, but they require considerable skill to be taken. Eagle watchers know from experience that one moment is filled with action and then there are long periods of quietness.

Strathspey. 26 December 1993. It's very cold, the temperature is -10°C and now that the fog is clearing a weak sun is trying to break through. It's taken me half an hour to ski up here from my car, over beautiful white powder snow, and I've passed deer and fox tracks on the way. Waited fifteen minutes but no sign of an eagle. I know they are there somewhere, but today it's too cold to wait.

The scattered spreading pines, stark against the snowy moorland, somehow remind me of the savannahs of East Africa. But here the temperature is well below freezing, and as I skied uphill, the birch trees beside the river were encased in hoarfrost. The scattered nature of the pines is not natural either: it's a forest in the last throes of death as a result of the historic destruction of the ancient forest of Caledon and in recent decades by overgrazing of tree seedlings by red deer.

Some red deer stags have scented me and nearly thirty have stopped briefly among the birches. The stags' breath freezes as puffs of mist in front of their noses. But still, no sign of an eagle.

In midwinter here the sun rises at about nine o'clock and sets again, over the hills, by four o'clock in the afternoon. It is a very short day in which to find enough food to last through the long, cold, winter nights of the Scottish Highlands. Even so, our golden eagles are permanent residents and this pair of adult birds will remain in their home range throughout the whole year, even during the worst days of winter. In other parts of the world, where the winters are even snowier and colder, golden eagles are migratory and move to

sunnier parts further south. In Scotland, easterly or northerly winds combined with high pressure give a very cold continental-like climate with snow and severe frosts. But when warm westerly winds blow in from the Atlantic, temperatures can rise up to ten degrees Celsius overnight. Then the snow melts, the ice on the lochs thaws, and the grass begins to grow in the fields. This odd combination of warm and cold weather enables eagles to remain here throughout the winter, making hunting easier in the warmer periods, yet at other times very difficult.

A dead red deer stag will provide food in winter for foxes, ravens, eagles and scavengers – in daytime they all give way to an adult golden eagle.

Eagles often rely on carrion in winter. Red deer and sheep die on the open hillsides and when stalkers are killing deer, from October to February, they leave the heads and stomach contents for scavenging birds such as ravens, crows and eagles. The alternative food is red grouse, ptarmigan and mountain hare. Unfortunately for the eagle, mountain hare and ptarmigan turn white in winter and become almost invisible when the land is covered with snow. But both have to feed, and the best places to find food during times of deep snow are on the exposed ridges where the wind has blown the snow from the ground. Eagles know this and will suddenly dive out of the sky and swoop across such places in the hope of a successful strike. When the snows have melted and the landscape is brown, the hare and ptarmigan stand out. Then they have a hard struggle to evade capture, while the richly marked red grouse is much less visible.

26 December 1992. A dark golden eagle is hunting the brown heather moorland hills to the south of the Tomintoul road as we walk towards Fae at 2.00 p.m. The grey clouds reveal some washed-out blue sky in the north, and there's a cold south wind coming off the hills towards the Ailnack River. The eagle is about 30 metres (100 ft) up, quartering west. The broad ends of the wings suddenly flick over on the wing tip and the bird plunges down with partly spread wings, missing a very white hare which had been hiding on a small snow wreath on the edge of burned heather. The mountain hare ran uphill but the eagle did not follow; instead it landed on the snow bank and just gazed around for eleven minutes. Forty red deer, in a loose group about 90 metres (300 ft) away, were more worried by our presence at five times the distance. Then the eagle took off and slowly circled westwards on the wind, rising up the hillside before disappearing.

So hunting is hard, but eagles seem to have ample time. If they do not catch food for one or even two days they can still manage. But they must also

19

Even long-dead animals
will provide a meal
for a hungry eagle.

An eagle tries to tear off a scrap of meat from a carcass.

cope with prolonged periods of blizzards, howling gales and wild wet nights of pouring rain. It is vital for eagles to know the best roosting places in their home range in order to keep dry and warm during the long nights of a Scottish winter. When sheets of icy cold rain pour on to the rock faces, it is vital to be under that dry overhang on the lee of the crags, safe from the elements. On another night the best roost is in the thickest tree at the edge of the Caledonian Forest, protected from biting wind and driving snow.

Often in winter I have looked at the old nests, seeming so dank and dead in January. The top of the eyrie is heaped with snow, the nest itself is grey and brown and sodden; it seems an unlikely place for a nest. Yet matters change dramatically in the spring, and the old nest can become a hive of activity in mid March.

There is little movement in the hills in January. Some winters ago, doing fieldwork for the British Trust for Ornithology winter atlas survey of birds in Great Britain, I walked to Glen Orrin in Easter Ross, a very remote glen surrounded by mountains. My job that day was to count numbers of birds of each species seen in a set time spent walking through each 10-kilometre (6-mile) square of country. I walked for six hours and all I saw was one snow bunting, one raven and six golden eagles.

Winter is usually a good time to see eagles. Fine, blue, spring-like days in February are best, especially if the previous week has been wet and windy. When wet snow-laden clouds have been pouring in from the north-west, no eagle is going to spend much time in the air; it would rather bed down in a secure roost. But when a beautiful fine day arrives this is the time to watch for eagles.

14 February 1994. I walked along one of the big sea lochs on the east coast of Harris in the Western Isles. There was a cold east wind blowing off the Minch and out to sea there were white tops to the waves and the few fishing boats working offshore were bucking into the wind. The land was surprisingly dry and I could walk over the frozen clumps of sphagnum and woolly hair moss.

At one stage I sat down against a grey rock and looked towards Tiumpan Head, while below me five eider ducks dived for mussels. A pair of golden eagles came soaring out from the low rocky hills on the other side of the sea loch. The male glided across the moor and landed on a small grey crag above a yellow grassy slope. Close behind him the female dropped lower and landed by a few stunted willow bushes on the heathery hillside. She shuffled around, ungainly, in the heather, and a minute or so later lifted a heather clump in her big talons. She slipped away down into a little gorge where she must have been building a nest. Within minutes she was back and flew to the same place to take another clump of dead heather. This time her mate followed a few hundred metres above and behind her but with no nest material.

I did not see them again until I was about a kilometre further down the coast. Looking back I could see the pair soaring high over the bleak wet heaths. It was good dry weather for nest building, with around a month left until egg laying.

This is the time of year when the red deer are down in the glens, packed together in big herds, waiting in some places for keepers to come with hay to feed them through the short winter days. It is the time when you see eagles flying fast and low across the land, intent on flushing a grouse from the peppered mix of tufts of heather sticking through a snowy landscape.

It is also a time when eagles die, especially young and inexperienced ones. Eagles will die if they do not find enough food or a secure place to roost. The juvenile birds are not allowed in the best territories, for the adult birds push them out to marginal areas where food is scarce and the proximity of man is an additional threat.

12 December 1971. Received a phone call from a local who had found a golden eagle in a fox trap on the moors, but had been unable to release it. He was calling from the Dorback telephone box. I arranged to meet him there as quickly as possible. The eagle was trapped well inside the hunting estate and we drove about 3 kilometres (2 miles) on a rough track behind Dorback Lodge before we reached the spot. The eagle was in a dreadful state, virtually comatose.

The traps had been set on a small hummock in a pool (at that time such traps were legal for foxes) and the bird was sodden, with just its head and wings out of the water. It had a gin trap on each leg, though only caught by one talon on each foot. I removed the bird quickly and we dried it in a sack and wrapped it in a duffel coat. As we drove along we kept the car heater blowing on the eagle, but it made little movement and we thought it would die. Stopping for petrol at a garage we met a motorist who had some brandy, so I gave the eagle a teaspoonful!

At home we kept the eagle above the Rayburn cooker in the kitchen. As it slowly dried out it started to open its eyes. After four hours there was a sudden improvement and the next look in the box showed that it had recovered. I kept it in a shed overnight and next day I gave it a brown hare. It refused to feed, probably because of the strange surroundings. Examination of the claws showed very little damage and the body condition was surprisingly good, so on the morning of 14 December I released it near Whitewells and it flew off very strongly towards Craigowrie.

Time to stand and stare.

22

An eagle soars up out of the glen;
in late winter and early spring
the male bird will often start
his roller coaster display when
he has gained enough height.

Dancing
in the
Skies

The rollercoaster display of a male golden eagle in spring is awe-inspiring, and each time I see it I am struck by its strength, grace and beauty. This is the sky dance of the eagle.

I remember one special time in Glen Affric, standing by an old dead Scots pine, and looking westwards up the loch towards the high mountains, still covered in snow. A pair of eagles came out of the corrie to the north and spiralled across the loch, until the female slowly dropped in a long glide into the big grey cliffs to the south. The male followed her for a while and then turned and gained height rapidly in the thermals, which were rising in the warm February sunshine from the northern side of the loch. In no time at all he was at least 300 metres (1000 ft) above me, maybe even 600 metres (2000 ft), when he reached his peak. Without warning he started to fall. He closed his wings and dived, but after 30 metres (100 ft) or so pulled out and swept upwards. This spectacular manoeuvre was repeated about ten times as he travelled westwards along the loch, then he banked and crossed the loch before performing the whole display again.

Undoubtedly his mate was watching him from below, but other eagles would have been watching as well. The next pair of eagles is only some 8 kilometres (5 miles) to the west; there is another pair in the forest the same distance to the east; to the south is a pair in the neighbouring glen; and a fourth by a big loch to the north. In these mountains in north Inverness-shire there are about fifty contiguous pairs of eagles.

The pair's home range consists of about 4,800 hectares (12,000acres) of land. These ranges have been handed down from generation to generation and seem to fit together like pieces of a great jigsaw. To the eagles this is their land, this is where they belong, where they give their display to show the next pair of eagles that this territory is occupied. On bright sunny days in spring every pair of eagles is showing their neighbours that they are ready to breed.

Within the home range each pair of eagles has one or more eyries, sometimes a series, used in different years. Usually, there are two, three or four nests, but there are records of up to fourteen nests in one home range, and I know of one pair of eagles with nine different nests. Occasionally a pair of eagles will have just one nest, which is used year after year, and this seems

A large eyrie in a granny Scots pine; often nests are very old and regular use and nest building means they can be two metres in height.

to happen more with a tree nest than with a crag nest.

As February gives way to March, the decision on nest choice will have been made. A sure sign that the birds have chosen a particular eyrie is to see the female perched on rocks or a pinnacle above the eyrie and the male bird soaring overhead. It is even better to see him dive out of the sky and land beside the female, or even mate with her on the rocks close to the nest.

The pair will already have started to refurbish the nest and the male will be bringing food to the female who spends more time near the chosen nest. Sometimes mating takes place some distance from the nest; a pair of birds will be gliding and following each other along the range of hills when the female lands on a big grey exposed rock. The male bird will fly slowly around her and then alight to mate.

Eagles live in many different habitats in Scotland. On the west coast and on the islands their nests are often in sea cliffs, maybe 30 or 60 metres (100 or 200 ft) high, the nest on a broad ledge facing out over the sea. Some ledges may have trees such as rowans and aspens which shade the nest during the summer time. At the bottom of the cliffs, a jumble of rocks may slope into the sea, a favourite place for otters to make their holts beneath big rocks and to fish along the shores for crabs and small fish. In the northern mountains of Sutherland and Wester Ross, and in Harris, broad stony deserts and scree-encrusted crags remind one of the Arctic. This is a landscape sculptured by glaciers. To the west, the mountains are grassier and eagles subsist on dead sheep and deer, and, in some places, on rabbits. On the rolling heather moors of the eastern Highlands wild prey is more plentiful, so many pairs build their big stick nests in ancient pines.

In one glen I know very well, a favourite pair of eagles has nested for at least fifteen years – I'm certain it was the same two birds throughout that time. They have six nests, all but one on the north-facing slope of the glen looking down over the public road. It is easy to look through a telescope mounted on the window of the car and see the female bird incubating on the nest. Another pair, to the north, has three nests along a series of cliffs that face east: one is small and tucked in behind a single rowan tree on the slope and I have never known it used in the dozen or so years I have watched them; their two main nests are in a tree-covered series of rocky ledges in a long cliff face. The next pair to the west has four nests, all very scattered; one huge nest used every few years is on the eagle's rock, Creag na h-Iolaire, a big dramatic rock face with scattered trees and big broad ledges. A kilometre or so to the north there are two nests on an isolated cliff face in a broad open glen, and to the

*With wings full spread, the eagle
searches the land below for prey.*

An immature eagle in flight
showing clearly the white base
to the tail which distinguishes
it from an adult bird.

south, also about a kilometre from the eagle's rock, is a very unusual nest built on top of a solitary rock on a bare, open hillside. We found it while doing a survey from a helicopter. The pair to the south has only two nests, one on a big rock face, about 90 metres (about 300 ft) high, and in the middle a big broad ledge with a very bulky nest indeed. About 20 metres (60 ft) to the side is a smaller nest, which I have never actually seen used.

Eagles can sometimes be inquisitive and look down on you as you climb in the mountains.

Such a pattern can be repeated all over Scotland, with various kinds of nests in different sorts of places, and pairs controlling varying numbers of nests. But in each area, if the pair is going to breed, one of the nests will be chosen early in the spring and repaired and renovated for use.

During the comprehensive survey of golden eagles breeding in Britain in 1982 by the RSPB and the Nature Conservancy Council, observers were asked to record details of nest sites for each pair of eagles that they visited. Jeff Watson and I analysed the data. The type of nest was recorded for 410 pairs, of which 96 per cent were on cliffs and 4 per cent in trees. All but one of the tree nests were in Scots pine; the other was in a larch. Among nests not used in 1982 were two in oaks. The distribution of tree nesting is heavily skewed to the east, with less than 1 per cent of pairs using trees in the western part of Scotland, but almost 10 per cent in the eastern part. Variation in amount of tree nesting is probably related to the fact that some of the largest native Scots pines still grow in the east, and the rounded hills of the eastern Highlands in any case often lack suitable nesting cliffs.

Throughout Europe, tree nests make up less than 10 per cent of the total, but after seeing a pair of eagles breeding in a woodland site in southern Sweden, I realised again that the distribution of eagles is often a result of man's interference and persecution. For in some parts of the world golden eagles still nest on flat and fertile lands associated with farming and human habitation, with villages quite close by. One such place is Skanör in southern Sweden, where a few pairs of eagles are nesting in close proximity to man. It is an area which I visited over a period of five years to collect young red kites from nests, under the guidance of Swedish ornithologists, so that we could restore the species as a breeding bird in Scotland.

Skanör. 4 April 1992. After visiting eleven red kite territories with Per-Olav Andersson, we sat on the edge of a field overlooking a broad valley. The valley is about 1 kilometre (0.6 miles) wide with wooded hill slopes to a depth of about 30 metres (100 ft) on both sides which level out to rolling rich agricultural plains

Carrying sticks to build up the eyrie is a regular activity in spring but even eagles sometimes play by dropping a piece of foliage and snatching it before it hits the ground.

dotted with beech woods and pine forests. The grey clouds of early morning were clearing and the lapwings were calling in the fields; a very pale buzzard sat on an alder tree beside the small river. As the sun came out, at least six buzzards soared up from the woods and started to display and they were joined by a male red kite, his beautiful chestnut tail showing up well in the sunlight.

Green woodpeckers yaffled from the woods; seven white wagtails in their dapper grey, black and white plumage landed in the grass and searched for insects among the cattle dung. Then some noisy crows on the far side heralded the arrival of a golden eagle. An immature bird, the flashes in his wings marked his progress through the trees and he landed on a dead elm in a small wood. Six hooded crows perched in the trees near him and continued their chivvying, but he ignored them and started to preen in the warm sun.

Skanör. 15 June 1993. Back at our favourite viewpoint; the evening sun is hot after the midday rain showers. Two roe deer are grazing in the lush meadows and a pair of lapwings has young. Icterine and marsh warblers sing their hearts out, while three cranes bugle further along the valley. We've collected ten young kites today and are tired. Lying on the warm bank drinking coffee, we have a superb view of a pair of adult golden eagles lazily flying along the wooded slopes opposite before gliding into the nesting wood. We're told they have young this year.

Were eagles given a chance they would breed again in many lowland wooded areas of Britain and other parts of Europe; though it might take a while for them to learn the habit of nesting in lowland woods again.

Golden eagles nest on cliffs at mean elevations of 150 metres (492 ft) above sea level in western Scotland and 450 metres (1476 ft) in eastern Scotland – not so far below the former treeline. There is a steady rise in height of the nests' locations from the western seaboard eastwards, with the highest nests recorded in the eastern Highlands. Perhaps the fact that there are fewer red grouse and mountain hare available in the mountains of the west means that eagles must hunt more low-ground prey, such as rabbits and seabirds. They prefer not to carry this prey a long distance up the hill to the nest, so it is advantageous to have the nests at lower altitudes. They also take sheep and deer carrion, easier to bring down rather than up to the nest. Eagles in the east, however, kill ptarmigan and mountain hares at higher altitude so it may be an advantage there to have the nest higher up the mountainside.

The situation elsewhere in Europe is comparable. In Norway the mean elevation of nests is between 500 and 600 metres (1640 and 1969 ft) and coincides closely with the natural treeline, where eagles hunt the open ground just above the trees. In contrast, the nest sites in the Alps and the Pyrenees are between 1500 and 1800 metres (4921 and 5906 ft) above sea level, where the eagles' favourite prey, the marmot, lives up on the alpine meadows. Marmots

Eagles are often harried by other species which live near them – crows, ravens, merlins and peregrine falcons are regular sparring partners.

A pair of adult golden eagles at their eyrie; in this case a rock ledge with a rowan tree growing to the front. Nests in Scotland are often placed behind such trees growing from rock ledges.

are now well distributed in these high mountains, though they were once very scarce because they were valued for their fat, used in the manufacture of cosmetics and for its healing properties. Once when travelling in the western mountains of Mongolia we stopped at some shepherds' yurts, and were offered a meal of marmots. A simmering pot over the fire was full of marmot stew, rather rabbit-like meat but incredibly greasy!

An adult golden eagle in flight.

Garmisch Partenkirchen. 10 May 1994. It is nearly five o'clock, a beautiful sunny afternoon with wispy white clouds and blue sky, now that the mountains are clearing. Up on the highest levels there are still some thick clouds remaining from the rain showers of midday. These mountains of the German alps are jagged and sheer chalky white. A golden eagle has just soared out from the top of the forest. It's a very dense, dark forest rising from the valley floor to meet the mountain cliffs. Where I stand, among the flower-studded alpine meadows with their old red-roofed wooden hay barns, there are a few apple trees with fresh green leaves and pinky-white flowers shining in the sun. Birch trees nestle among the lower spruce trees but as the wood reaches higher and higher, stretching for maybe 1 kilometre (0.6 miles) above me, it becomes solely spruces. Then it's 500 metres (1640 ft) or more to the top of the cliffs.

The eagle flew out from the treeline. I expect she has a nest in a hole or a cavern in the cliff face. She soared effortlessly round and round, slowly gaining height. There's a notch about halfway along her right wing and just the faintest signs of white patches still in her wings: she is a sub-adult bird. Five minutes later she disappears into the misty clouds above the highest cliffs. In all the time that I have watched her through my binoculars she has not flapped her wings once. She just gently spiralled upwards on the warm air rising from the rocks and blown into the mountains from the west.

The blue and white rack railway from the glacier ski lift has just passed me on its way down to the village. Further up to my right are the lifts which carry skiers into the mountains in wintertime. As I look up to where the eagle started her flight there seemed to be no tracks, just steep forest rising at sixty degrees or more. Above that the jagged rocks rise to the alpine meadows. That's where the eagles go hunting for marmots – out in the spring sun after their winter's hibernation.

In contrast the golden eagles breeding on the east European plains live at low level in forests, marshes and farmland stretching from the eastern part of Germany through to Russia. There they live alongside other forest nesting raptors such as greater and lesser spotted eagles.

Poland. 29 May 1985. On the edge of the Red Moss in north-east Poland looking across this incredibly flat plain. A marsh spreads as far as I can see, with scattered silver-stemmed birches growing in the foreground and on the slightly drier hillocks across the moss. In other places, squelching marshland, knee-deep with sedges, holds rare birds such as great snipe and aquatic warblers. A Montagu's harrier has just flown by, a beautiful male with black and grey plumage.

As we walk back from the marshy plain we enter the most superb primeval pine forest. A black woodpecker calls in the distance, there are big heaps of wood ant nests, and the loveliest of forest bogs. In one of the clearings is a really nice pool, 200 metres (656 ft) across, linked by a stream to a bog full of willow bushes. There is evidence of beavers, and at one end, where the little river attempts to flow out of the pond, there's a huge beaver lodge: a great pile of sticks, 1.8 metres (6 ft) high and 3.6 metres (12 ft) across, where the beavers have built their home.

Looking back over the pond, over the top of the beavers' lodge, which undoubtedly had a family of beavers inside keeping well clear of our noisy approach through the forest, I saw a pair of golden eagles spiral up out of the pine wood. Our forest guide told me they were nesting in the forest. These birds would feed on a range of different prey, but mainly birds such as black grouse, hazel hen and capercaillie, as well as ducks, coots and wading birds from the Red Moss.

In Scotland, we found that the majority of nests faced between north-west and east, while only a few had their nests facing between west and south-east. Eagles in Scotland prefer nests with a northerly rather than a southerly aspect. They choose sites which provide maximum protection from the prevailing wet weather (which mainly comes from the south-west) and to avoid excessive exposure to sun to reduce the risk of nestlings overheating. This may seem an odd problem in the wet summers we often experience in Scotland, but when it is hot, south-facing rock ledges become very hot indeed, and young eagles can be seen panting hard to keep cool.

Continuing with the results of the 1982 survey, we checked the distance to the nearest public road and found that 31 nests out of a sample of 406 were within 1 kilometre (0.6 miles) of a public road. At the other extreme there were at least 30 nests further than 8 kilometres (5 miles) from a public road. We found no indication that distance from a public road had any effect on the degree of success or failure of a nest, although there have been occasions when birds have deserted a home range because of an increase in disturbance relating to use of roads.

Observers were asked to score the accessibility of nests in three bands of difficulty. Was the eyrie easy to climb into; very difficult, needing a rope; or impossible to get to? We found that the pairs which used nest sites that were easily accessible to people were more likely to fail completely than were pairs using inaccessible eyries. It is obviously much easier for egg collectors and people who destroy eagles' eggs and young to get to the more accessible nests. Easily reached eyries would also be vulnerable to disturbance or damage by pine martens, foxes, or even trampling by sheep or goats, but we believe that disturbance by people was the principal reason for failure.

An eagle hunts across heather slopes. Sharp eyes, speed and stealth give it the best chance of catching an unwary red grouse or mountain hare, but even for an eagle, hunting is hard work and often unsuccessful.

A newly hatched eaglet, its head covered in spiky white down.

Early Life in the Eyrie

Although some eyries in Scotland are only a quarter of an hour's walk from the road, or may even be viewed with a telescope from the comfort of the car, other nests are some kilometres off the beaten track. Checking eagle nests in the springtime is pure magic: walking into the back of the mountains in Inverness-shire and standing on the high tops looking out over range after range of incredible scenery to the Minch glistening in the distance.

Often the nesting cliff may be visible for several kilometres, but as you tramp up the glen, passing the stumps of ancient forests and wading across burns, there seems to be no evidence of eagles, let alone a nest. The male bird may be away hunting, or perched in a roosting site well out of view, while his female sits tight on the nest. Some eagles will not leave their nests during incubation, however close a human observer may come. None the less, I would not visit a nest in bad weather, in case the eagle is disturbed and the eggs become chilled.

The busiest time at an eagles' eyrie is just before egg laying. The birds are actively nest building during the day. You may see one of them drift over, lift a stick or heather bush from the ground and drag it back to the nest. Sometimes it will swoop down to break a branch off a dead tree and lumber back towards the nest with a stick about 1 metre (3.2 ft) long trailing behind it. It is surprising how quickly they build, hurrying back and forth, bringing another stick to the nest every few minutes.

You may also see the female gathering nesting material for the centre of the nest; the favourite is the greater woodrush. On several occasions I have seen a female land on a cliff thick with woodrush and watched her stumble around in the long green and yellow vegetation, trying to tear out bits by the roots. Sometimes she would fly out from the cliff to dislodge a particularly tough clump. The eagle then flies back to the nest with what looks like a big shopping basket under her tail. Once the woodrush is trodden into the base of the nest and woven in by the female's bill, it forms an extremely warm and comfortable bed for her eggs.

Some nests are well sheltered by overhanging rocks. There is one in Wester Ross, where I climbed up through a gorge and could see no sign of a suitable place for the eagles' nest I had heard was there. I turned a corner suddenly and there was a hidden rock face, perhaps 15 metres (50 ft) high and 30 metres (100 ft) long, on a right-angled bend of the gorge with the river running below

The male eagle arrives at the eyrie but has failed to bring food for the hungry chick.

it. Half a dozen rowan trees were growing on the crags, safe from the gnawing teeth of red deer and sheep, and close to the top of the crags was the eagles' nest, under the most superb overhanging rock. At the northern end was an old, gnarled, stunted rowan tree, three or four stems growing upright, another fallen over at right angles, providing an excellent horizontal perch for the birds.

Usually when we were checking eagle nests in the spring, as part of the monitoring work that we did for the RSPB, we would be visiting nests that had been known for many years, in some cases for over a century. We had to establish whether or not the pair of eagles was present, whether they were breeding, and which nest was in use, and, later in the season, how many young were reared. This was the basic information required for our conservation work.

But in ranges where we had no previous knowledge of the places where eagles were nesting we would need to cold search. First we would watch the birds, hoping that their activities would lead us to their nests. Sometimes we would go to vantage points and use binoculars and telescopes to search for suitable nesting sites. Eventually, we could almost think like an eagle, and knew where to look for the nests. At times it was quite uncanny to explore a new glen and judge where the best place for a nest would be, and walk several kilometres to find one in that precise spot.

Occasionally we found eyries in places which had not been used for many years. New eagle pairs had recolonised areas deserted for many decades due to persecution. In the early 1980s I found a pair at a site where the locals had told me they had not nested for over fifty years. When I climbed up to the newly built nest I found the remains of an ancient eyrie underneath. And, in the jumble of rocks below the crag, I found an old hide where long, long ago gamekeepers would have hidden and shot at the birds as they came to the nest.

The tell-tale sign of yellow lichen staining the rock below an ancient nesting site suggests that eagles have used it in the distant past. Some nests are extremely old and several in northern Inverness-shire are immense. One was in an ancient Scots pine tree; the keepers told me it had been there long before they could remember. I have a photograph of this nest with one of my colleagues, Bob Swann, climbing the tree to ring the youngster. The huge nest was larger than he was. This particular nest is only used every five years or so, so it must have been constructed over many decades. Chris Mylne filmed there in 1961 for an RSPB film, and the tree nowadays looks no different from how it did then. The tree itself is well over 200 years old.

Eventually massive nests collapse: they either topple over or become too

As the young start to grow, the parents break off fresh foliage from nearby trees and bring it to the eyrie as decoration.

39

heavy for the branch to support. I first saw this when I found a nest in an old Scots pine. I was aware there had been a nest in that area but had never managed to locate it.

Inverness-shire. 8 May 1978. It was a bright morning not long after dawn, I was hiking along the top of the forest and disturbed an eagle out of the wood. As I walked into the wood I could see that it had been well used by eagles, for in several places under their roosting sites I found freshly moulted feathers and down, as well as a few feathers of red grouse, which they had plucked.

Walking on through the wood I suddenly discovered a huge nest high up in the tree. I looked up with my binoculars and was amazed, because the nest itself was supported by two great spars of timber wood. It was an artificial nest, but who built it and how long ago?

Later that day I spoke to the forest ranger and he remembered that in the 1930s, when he was a child, his father had helped Seton Gordon build the artificial nest. Seton had been visiting the original nest on and off over the years, but when he returned one spring he found that it had become too heavy for the branch, which had snapped, and the nest had tipped to the ground. Seton Gordon had persuaded a couple of locals to help him rebuild the eyrie.

Later in the summer we climbed to that nest to ring the youngster and, hanging on the branch above, we found an old wooden pulley, which Seton and his friends had secured in order to pull up those great spars to support the nest. Years afterwards I found the pulley on the ground; the rope had finally rotted and it had fallen down. I took it home and it sits proudly in my office as a memento of this extraordinary nest.

Just as Seton Gordon rebuilt an eagle's nest, so the RSPB has been constructing nest sites for eagles. One of my friends in the RSPB built two nests, not far from where I live, to persuade a pair of golden eagles to move from a nest rather close to a public road. The following year, the eagles noticed the new nests and moved to one of them. They look just like natural nests and both have been used in successive years to rear the young eagles away from disturbance.

In Scotland, most eggs are laid from mid March onwards, although a few pairs will have laid their eggs as early as the end of the first week of March. Just before egg laying, the pair of birds spend most of their time near the nest. It is very noticeable that the male keeps in close contact with his mate during this time and the pair are frequently seen flying together in harmony and almost always in sight of the nest area.

The first egg is laid, and a second, rarely a third, will be laid two to four days later. The new eggs are beautiful, their creamy-white background decorated with reddish-brown flecks or spots. They are large, about the size of a small goose egg, heavy, thick-shelled, and very sturdy-looking. I have a photograph of a pair of eggs in a beautiful soft nest made of woodrush; the green stems have withered among the yellow-brown clumps from the previous year, and dotted among them are little white puffy down feathers from the eagle's breast. It looks a really comfortable nest in which to sit – probably just as well, because

When the chicks are young the female spends the night keeping them warm in the eyrie while the male eagle roosts in a nearby tree.

41

The female grabs foliage for nest lining from a rowan tree growing on the slope opposite her eyrie.

it will take six weeks of incubation before the eggs hatch.

Sometimes both eggs are marked with brown, but not often, and they may not be marked with the same patterns. One may be speckled all over with reddish-brown, while the other may be whiter, with big brown blotches on one end and occasional markings across the rest of the shell. Each female lays eggs of a characteristic nature and it is possible for someone who is studying a particular eyrie to recognise a change of female. In the past, people who took eggs for collections also recognised this, and some collectors delighted in having a series of clutches from the same female, dating back a decade or more.

The female eagle sits very tightly after the first egg is laid. The eggs are warmed against the 'brood patch' of bare skin on her belly. She is given short rests by the male, giving her a chance to feed, but it is her job to sit throughout the night. Sometimes she requires to sit through periods of snow, throwing it off with a shake of her wings. When snow is very heavy and the wind is blowing from the wrong direction, the nest becomes so thickly covered that she is forced to leave the nest and eggs. Once or twice during my years in the hills I have found a nest with the eggs left in the cup after heavy falls of snow have forced a desertion.

Inverness-shire. 29 March 1985. Colin Crooke and I went early to Cannich to check a nest which we thought had been robbed by egg thieves. After talking with the foresters, we walked to the two tree eyries and saw the marks of climbing irons up both of the nest trees. Fortunately neither nest was in use that year. We noticed the movement of a female eagle gliding towards the cliffs about 400 metres (1300 ft) above us on the slope. She had not seen us, because we were under the trees, and as we watched, she landed on the edge of a bulky nest in a small grey cliff. Almost immediately the male bird rose up and slipped out past the female and away along the cliffs, and she shuffled in and sat on her eggs.

When we climbed to the eyrie, the female flew off and we found two well-marked eggs surrounded by snow. We marked both eggs, using an invisible security pen, in case the egg thieves returned. As we returned down the glen the female was seen to go back to the nest.

When the young are several weeks of age, the female perches in a nearby Scots pine and watches her young from a distance without being pestered by them.

It is rare for there to be more than two eggs in a nest, sometimes there is only one, but there are records in Scotland of a pair of golden eagles managing to rear broods of three young at one time. In 1979 a nest which we had regularly watched over the years, in a big pine tree in one of the north Inverness glens, contained four eggs, two of which hatched successfully. This is an extremely large clutch to find in a golden eagle eyrie but we decided in the end that there may have been two females involved.

42

Even at an early age the older chick is threatening the smaller one and driving it from the centre of the nest. Smaller chicks often perish through lack of food and constant bullying.

Inverness-shire. 25 May 1980. I visited the site with my son, Gavin. As we approached the nesting area I saw two eagles against the hillside, so I was quite sure I would find the nest in use. But when we reached the big eyrie in the Scots pine, which had four eggs the previous year, and I had climbed up above it on the hillside to look in, I could see only two eggs. The nest was obviously still in use and there was fresh green pine foliage and white down on the nest. The two birds were still present and one was coming quite close to us and occasionally calling. I was surprised the birds were still showing so much attention to a nest containing eggs, which I thought must now be addled.

As we were sitting near the nest I heard a young eagle call a short distance away, and with my binoculars scanned a small wooded cliff about 90 metres (300 ft) from the tree eyrie. There I saw a nest, a new eyrie, which I had not previously been aware of. We clambered across to it and found a well-built-up nest containing two youngsters of about three weeks old; there was fresh food in the nest and the birds were obviously thriving.

Later we returned to ring the two young. At the time of ringing, the addled eggs were still in the other nest and three adult golden eagles were in the sky overhead. We were convinced that the male had mated with two different females, one female laying in each of the nests. Cases of bigamy in golden eagles are extremely rare and there have been no previous references to it in the British Isles, although cases have been reported in Europe.

For the second half of March and most of April eagles are incubating and it is a quiet time at the nests. The male bird is hunting, sometimes bringing food, and occasionally allowing the female to go off and hunt while he incubates.

At one of the nests we were able to watch carefully, we found that the amount of incubation by the male changed from year to year. In 1984 and 1985 the female spent three times longer incubating during the day than the male, but in 1986 the male was on the eggs only a little less than the female. The female, however, spends all night on the eggs.

It is interesting to observe the difference in behaviour of the two birds when changing duties at the eyrie. When the female came back to the nest she invariably took a few minutes to tidy the nest or rearrange some sticks or rushes on the edge of the eyrie, and then walked gently onto the nest. When the male arrived, he immediately pushed her out of the way and settled on the eggs!

It is extremely touching to watch an eagle alight on its nest. The huge talons might damage the eggs, so before settling, the eagle carefully closes them into a fist, so that they can do no harm. Then it gently lowers itself down. Finally, it rocks around, getting the eggs in a comfortable position against the brood patch among the feathers on its belly. During a long stint of incubation eagles usually get up after about an hour or so, to ease their feathers and stretch their legs, to adjust their position, and to turn the eggs.

In 1971 the pair of eagles nesting in the Lake District, guarded by the RSPB, were watched carefully by the wardens who made detailed notes of which bird was incubating throughout the day and night. Incubation of the first egg started on 26 March and one eaglet hatched on 3 May. The male participated in incubation on thirty-two of the thirty-eight days of incubation and, overall, he had accounted for 6 per cent of the whole incubation stint. Over the whole period no other particular pattern emerged for the male's share in incubation. The observers usually found it impossible to deduce why a changeover had taken place: it was not clearly linked to the male arriving with food, though on some changeovers the male arrived with some nest material. Changes were often accompanied by much calling by both eagles. It was difficult to avoid the impression that this particular male had a great urge to play his part in incubation, for at least once he nudged the female off the eggs, and on another occasion the female failed to budge him from the eggs when she returned to the nest.

At most eagle nests this daily routine continues uninterrupted through the incubation period, with variety provided by dramatic changes in weather as well as skirmishes with local ravens and peregrines. Problems during incubation are usually due to illegal persecution, such as egg robberies and the killing of the adults.

Nevertheless, at one Cannich nest the theft of eggs (and subsequent apprehension of the collectors) threw up a new fact about golden eagles. In late May we realised the pair was busy in another part of its home range and, on 31 May, a new nest containing a three-day-old chick and one egg was found. It was about 3.5 kilometres (2.2 miles) from the original robbed site. The second egg did not hatch, but the single chick thrived and I ringed it on 27 June and it flew successfully. This pair of eagles had laid a replacement clutch of eggs, the first time that this has been definitely recorded in the British Isles.

Some eagles are still shot in their nests and some people destroy eggs by dropping rocks into nests, or will even deliberately set fire to eyries. Fortunately these dreadful acts are becoming less frequent as more people come to cherish eagles. The annual burning of heather in spring is still a problem for nesting eagles. Muirburning, practised correctly, is an accepted part of range management but too often it is a haphazard affair. Fires get out of control and others are left to burn unguarded. Sometimes huge areas are burned and fires can last for days. I remember a fire in north Sutherland which burned much of the home range of one pair of eagles and part of another's.

On one occasion, in April 1981, the fire was closer to home, where a colleague from the RSPB was filming eagles. The sporting tenant, who did not live in the area, was up on holiday and set fire to the heather low in the glen. The fresh wind carried the fire up the hillside on to neighbouring land and soon the whole mountain was consumed by smoke. Despite the efforts of the fire brigade and Forestry Commission staff the fire was difficult to control. All the eagle crags were burned and the nest had smoke billowing from around it as we trudged downhill at dusk. I do not know how long the hen sat against the onslaught of fire and smoke. But when we checked the next day it was clear she had deserted. All the vegetation around the nesting cliff had been burned and, although the nest itself had not caught fire, it had clearly been too much for her to take.

Sometimes eyries become so large they crash out of the tree during storms.

Eaglets in the Eyrie

The young eagle begins to call to its parents from inside the egg several days before the hatch. The first egg laid will hatch two, perhaps three, days before the second. When the chick starts to break its way out of the egg it uses the tiny sharp white egg 'tooth' on the tip of the upper mandible to crack the egg from the inside. At the same time it starts to rotate inside the egg, slowly chipping its way out of the shell.

This is a testing time for the young chick. It can take twenty-four hours before it breaks the shell sufficiently to flex its stubby wings and legs and push itself clear of the egg. The female knows what is happening during this time, for she can feel the young chick stirring beneath her. Once the little creature is dry, it is quite beautiful. Pure fluffy white, its wings are hardly visible, just blunt little stumps. Its legs, which will be huge and yellow with black talons when adult, are tiny and flesh-coloured, while the tiny bill is bluish, with a black tip and a noticeable little white egg 'tooth' on the end which will disappear in a matter of days. The fleshy gape and the flesh around the top of the bill and nostrils are soft pink and the dark brown eye is surrounded by a grey area of skin. The white fur is very spiky; a dense white warm undercoat has longer hairs which stick up to give it a 'punkish' look.

Once the first egg hatches, the female leaves the nest more regularly and can be away for ten to twenty minutes, perching and preening nearby on the crags. She is not evidently concerned about the chick in the second egg because it is already fully formed and able to regulate its own body heat.

A friend made some observations at a nest in the mid 1980s, and found that the first egg hatched on 28 April 1984. On that day, the female was off the nest for two short periods in the afternoon. By the 29th, when the second chick hatched, she was off for exactly one hour during the afternoon. At the same nest in 1985, the first egg hatched on 21 April, and on the 22nd, during a period of cold wet mist, she sat continuously in the morning for a four-and-a-half-hour stint, but later in the afternoon she was off for five minutes, then ten and finally fourteen minutes, when the mist cleared to reveal a weak sun. In the following year the first egg hatched on 19 April and by the 20th she was off for six minutes and twenty minutes at a time. The progressively earlier hatching dates are part of a remarkably normal pattern: the older birds tend to breed earlier, probably due to their knowledge of the local habitat and feeding conditions.

A female feeding her young during a rain shower.

When the second chick hatches, its older sibling will already be a good deal larger. Both chicks need to be fed and cared for, and now there is a change in the behaviour of both parents. The female's job is now to protect her chicks from predators, which might attack them in the nest, as well as from the weather. During the night and when it is cold or wet, she will brood them under her warm body. In some parts of the world there is the risk of eaglets overheating, so the female will stand over them with her wings outspread to prevent the sun striking them during the hottest time of the day.

The male bird has to provision the nest for the growing young. If he has caught a grouse, he plucks the carcase, flies into the nest and presents his mate with the food. She tears up the grouse and gently feeds the young with very small pieces of meat. In no time at all she is gently clucking and persuading the tiny chicks to open their bills for food. Any large bits, too difficult for the young to eat, will be eaten by the female.

Ross-shire. 24 April 1982. With Mike Richards and Alister Brebner went to the eyrie where the RSPB were filming. It was midday by the time we climbed the deer path. The male, still with a gap in one of his wings, flew off early, mobbed by five crows. As we approached the photographic hide the female left the eyrie where she had been sitting tight. A three-day-old chick was in the nest, with a dud egg. The remains of two freshly killed red grouse and an adult weasel were in the nest. The tiny eaglet was very perky and took a small piece of meat which I offered it. Mike got in the hide for a spell of filming. Alister and I went back down the cliffs, as decoys, and by the time we reached the river both eagles were back near the nest, although a cock merlin was chivvying them. So to check the second pair.

After a lengthy walk up the glen, I reached the base of the crags and after scrambling about the ledges for ten minutes I disturbed a female from a new eyrie with chick(s). It was impossible to look into the nest; even with a rope it would have been a struggle, but I heard a chick cheeping. There was the white wing of a ptarmigan under the ledge and the signs and smell of a fox having searched the same place for scraps (foxes often search the ground below eagle nests for food remains). The female came back to the nest within five minutes, and with my telescope I had fantastic close views – she had an unusual pupil to her eye which was more like the funny shape of a pigeon's.

The chicks grow quickly and after a week the pure whiteness of the first down becomes greyer, and they do not look quite as appealing as on those first few days. They are also smelly and dirty, because at this stage they cannot clean themselves or preen properly, and the female is feeding them with bloody prey freshly brought in by the male. The head and bill, and sometimes the rest of the body, are clammy with blood.

The bigger, normally the more active, older chick is likely to get most of the food. When food is scarce he or she will monopolise what there is, and is always there first to take food from the female. This happens often in Scotland, where males can find it difficult to catch enough food to rear two

The larger chick bullied the smaller, took most of the food from the female and in the end was the sole survivor at this eyrie.

The red grouse is a famous bird of the heather moors of Scotland and is a favourite prey for the golden eagle.

chicks. The parents do not share out the food but feed the larger until it is full. Observers in hides close to nests have seen females feed one chick up to fifty times more than another when food is scarce.

When they are not feeding or sleeping, the older chicks often bully the younger. They will pursue their hapless sibling around the nest, only allowing it a rest when food arrives or when the smaller one cowers motionless out on the edge of the nest. The parents do not intervene. As the youngster gets weaker its older brother or sister becomes more aggressive towards it. Sometimes this is manifested by continual pecking of the back of the smaller chick's head, removing the down and exposing bare skin, even causing bleeding. Sometimes the smaller chick is killed or pushed out of the eyrie, but in many cases it simply dies from starvation. Some eagle species exhibit extreme sibling aggression: they lay two eggs but only one chick ever survives. The reason for this is not clear.

In Scotland only about 15 per cent of nests manage to rear two young. Usually these are in areas with a higher density of live prey, and some pairs regularly rear two young year after year. There is a favourite nest of mine in Easter Ross where the parents reared two chicks four years out of five. They were such good hunters, and the food supply in that home range was so plentiful, that they had no problem in supplying enough food for two young.

In May the chicks should be growing well, the weather is improving and there are some lovely sunny days in the Highlands. The male bird is bringing a good variety of prey to the nest. It is easy to see when a young eagle is well fed, because its crop is bulging, yet in a few hours' time it will have digested all that food. When the crop is full it looks like a large tennis ball stuck to its breast. But when eaglets are hungry they look very hollow-chested and the folds in the skin are visible.

Ross-shire. 15 May 1980. Two well-grown youngsters, about a month old, in the nest and in beautiful condition: bright-eyed and busy-looking. The nest was filled like a larder, with eight red grouse carcases, mostly females, and at least half completely plucked by the male eagle and ready to eat. Two had been half eaten; there was also a full-grown blue hare and a stoat. I looked down at this feast and thought that when I got home that evening we'd probably have minced beef and tatties. I was tempted to take a couple of the grouse home for dinner.

Later, in the winter, when I was reading an old book about ancient times in the Highlands, I came across a reference to the fact that several hundred

The hunt is always on when young eagles are in the eyrie, the male has to search far and wide in his home range to find enough prey.

Even when the eaglet is quite large, the female still tears up the food and feeds her youngster in a most delicate manner. The male has had good hunting and this eyrie is well provisioned.

years ago, when life in the Highlands was far from easy, some people had learned that they could take food from eagles' nests. Living in the glens was a hard struggle for existence, with large families living in awful conditions, often with very little to eat. The older boys used to climb up the rocks to the eyries and remove some of the food in the nest. It would have been a great day for a young lad to walk home with six red grouse and a blue hare to present to his mother to feed her hungry family. This custom is also known from other parts of the world and there are even records of cases where young eaglets were tethered to the nest for an extra two or three weeks to ensure the continued supply of food.

Eagles seem to have incredible patience, standing or sitting doing nothing for hour after hour. The young are well fed and asleep, and yet the female cannot leave them, for she has to make certain they are not harmed. Occasionally she will fly off and tear green sprays from trees growing in the cliffs and will bring back fronds of fresh aspen, birch or pine to decorate the nest. She seems to be spring cleaning it. As more and more prey is brought in, the nests become unpleasantly dirty and undoubtedly the fresh vegetation improves matters. It also adds to the bulk of the nest, and the larger the nest and the more securely it is made, the longer it will survive.

After three weeks the first black feathers start to show through the eaglet's white down. The bill grows firm, the area around its base turns yellow and the feet are growing fast and gaining strength as they also turn yellow. The black talons are starting to harden. The body of the eaglet grows first; the wings take longer, most of their growth taking place in the second half of the time that the young eaglet is in the nest.

By now the eaglets are getting quite aggressive. At a human's approach they will puff themselves up, spread their wings, open their bills and threaten menacingly. They are also more active, and walk around the nest picking at vegetation or bits of food. The female is still regularly feeding them and the male still brings food to the nest. If there is too much food in the nest, the female may lift a carcass, fly a short distance away from the nest and poke it in among the vegetation on a cliff ledge, making a sort of larder or cache that she can visit later. Some birds do this more often than others.

As well as carrion, such as dead lamb and deer, eagles will also kill roe deer fawns and young red deer calves and carry them back to the nest. There is a whole range of chance food.

Strathspey. 19 June 1994. In the evening I went to the eagles' eyrie not far from home. I climbed the big Scots pine to ring the two chicks. Both were thriving, one's outer wing measured 320 mm (12.6 in), the other 315 mm (12.4 in). There were two dead red squirrels in the eyrie, one male, one female, neither yet eaten. These must have been caught recently in the open pine forest nearby. The younger chick had been eating a female red grouse, and there was a mountain hare skin and also a common shrew.

I have seen stoat and weasel as well as fox cubs in the nest. Sometimes

these cubs have been caught and killed as they played outside their dens, but I remember gamekeepers in the mountains telling me that they have killed foxes at dens and laid the carcases on a rock from where an eagle has taken them.

Eagles will even catch food as small as water voles. In the Highlands the water voles of the mountain streams are black and it is surprising how many the eagles will catch. They also catch frogs and small songbirds. Lea MacNally told me about an eagle chick he was studying one year. One week late in the season the only food it received from its parents was meadow pipit nestlings. These tiny morsels could not do much for an eagle chick; it seemed rather like feeding only sweets to a growing child.

Throughout the world, eagles are opportunists and will hunt whatever is equivalent to the red grouse and mountain hare of Scotland. In North America, cottontails, jackrabbits, ground squirrels and sage grouse are captured, while in mainland Europe, willow grouse, hares, marmots and susliks are favourite prey. In Mediterranean countries tortoises are a common prey.

Dadia Reserve, Greece. Monday 8 May 1989. I am in eastern Greece near the Turkish border and just to the west of the Evros River, a superb area for birds of prey. Twenty-four species of raptors breed here and another ten come to winter or pass through on migration. This is the most diverse population of raptors in Europe; in fact 90 per cent of European raptor species occur here. About twenty pairs of golden eagles nest in the forested hills of the reserve, and other eagles which nest here include booted, Bonelli's, lesser spotted, imperial, white-tailed and short-toed eagles.

In the morning I went with Kostas Pistolas, one of the rangers in charge of the reserve, and a couple of his colleagues to look at a long-legged buzzard's nest. Then we drove up a rough track on to a rocky hillside and walked across a sandy plain dotted with big rocks and stunted pine trees. Skirting along the top of the ridge we looked down into an old gnarled Scots pine and saw a female golden eagle feeding her young on the nest. The youngster was about two weeks old, white and fluffy and very alert. The adult bird soon saw us and flew off through the trees towards the north.

Looking below the nest we saw the remains of tortoises, and it was a tortoise that the bird had been feeding to her young. The golden eagles get at the flesh by dropping the tortoises from a height and breaking their shells against the rocks. As we walked back to our car we came across a couple of live tortoises, beautifully marked with diamonds of black against a greeny olive shell. We also came across the parched remains of tortoise shells broken on rocks by the eagles; at least seven tortoises had been killed.

We drove about three kilometres (two miles) to a viewpoint where we sat to eat our lunch and had good views of griffon vultures on a rock face where they were starting to nest. Further away, towards where we had seen the eagles nesting, I saw a golden eagle dropping a tortoise. The bird was 70 to 90 metres (200 to 300 ft) above the hillside and I could clearly see it drop a football-like object from its talons to fall to the rocks below. It repeated the process twice. A couple of

When there is a glut of food at the eyrie, adults occasionally take older remains away to eat later (top).
The male eagle arrives with a grouse at the eyrie.

short-toed eagles drifted across the valley heading for open land where they searched for snakes and far in the distance, over several wooded ridges, one of the adult sea eagles drifted up and soared above its old nest site, not used this year. Before we left, a hobby was seen chasing dragonflies, and a brightly coloured hoopoe carried a small lizard back to its family in a dead tree.

The Greek poet and dramatist Aeschylus, who lived in the fifth century BC, died after a tortoise was dropped on his head, presumably by an eagle. More recently, Israeli ornithologists studied a pair of golden eagles near Jerusalem during the nesting season and saw them kill no fewer than eighty-four tortoises, dropped from heights of 30-70 metres (100-230 ft) – sometimes as many as eight times before the shell broke open.

By six weeks, the young eagle is starting to look like its parents. Much of the body is covered in dark brown feathers, the head is still white and some down is still present. The wing feathers are growing well, the tail is starting to sprout and the bird is able to grasp prey brought in by its parents, and to feed itself. The female is spending more time away from the nest and is hunting more.

Even when two-thirds grown, eaglets can die if there is a shortage of food, which can happen in some summers even when both adults are hunting. If two chicks have survived to this stage, one of them may die from lack of food, slowly getting weaker and in the end starving to death. I have known cases where a solitary youngster has died in the nest not long before it was due to fly, but, in general, once they are over half grown they are fairly secure.

The big feathers of the wings and tail are the last to grow; these are the major feathers that will carry the bird aloft. Each feather takes several weeks to complete. If young birds go hungry at this stage, the feather growth is checked and fault bars appear. These are weak points which may be a problem in the future, for a particularly weak feather may break. As each feather comes out of its waxy sheath, the bird spends time gently preening it with its bill and removing the casing.

On the few occasions when I have watched the chicks close up, I have always been struck by how much time they spend just gazing around. They scan the sky eagerly for any sign of their parents returning with food, but they also watch the local hooded crows fly by, or maybe a high-flying gull or heron. Sometimes a wren or a chaffinch will land on the edge of the nest or in the trees close to the eyrie. All of these will be watched with great interest as part of growing up. They also watch the weather; they see their first snow falling, they will know what heavy rain is, they see the sun rising in the mountains and setting in the north-west. They will note the very short nights of the summer in Scotland with just that darkening between 11.30 p.m. and 2.00 a.m., when the sun barely sinks below the northern horizon. All through those nights it is clear enough for an eagle to see. They will learn to recognise the stars and the rising of the moon. All these things will tell the eagle where its home is in the Scottish Highlands.

Large young calling for food – at this stage young eaglets can be surprisingly noisy but later in life golden eagles are generally silent.

58

Learning to Fly

Wing flapping is extremely important for young birds of prey, because they need to strengthen their wing muscles in preparation for flight. Their future will depend on the ability to fly. At around six or seven weeks old they become more active as the downy feathers on their heads fall away and their bodies approach full size. The main wing feathers still have a long way to grow, so there is still no chance of the bird rising off the nest.

Parent birds can be hit by the beating wings of the young so they will spend less time in the nest now to avoid congestion. The shape of the nest has changed by this time: it is broad and flat, for the cup that was there for the eggs has gone. The new foliage placed continually on the eyrie by the parents has flattened it out; it is an ideal base for youngsters to walk around, test their wings and feed on scraps.

At this stage, we visit nests to ring the young in order to follow their movements and learn more about their ecology. However, many nests are impossible to get to so most eagle chicks are not ringed.

One person usually stays at the top of the cliff, or the bottom of the tree, while the other climbs to the nest and retrieves the eaglet in a sack, so that we can ring it safely on level ground. Eagle rings, at 26 mm (1 in) internal diameter, are the largest produced by the ringing scheme of the British Trust for Ornithology. They are now made from a very hard Monel metal, for we were sure that the softer aluminium rings we once used were occasionally pulled off the leg by an eagle when tearing up its prey. At the time of ringing we take measurements of the length of the wings and the weight of the chick. We have sometimes also placed a coloured ring on the other leg, and, for a short time in the 1980s, a few of us marked eaglets with brightly coloured wing tags, which allowed us to identify the birds, using a telescope, during the wintertime.

Strathspey. 4 July 1960. I ringed my first eagle. A glorious day, a little high cloud; it was warm and after an early breakfast we set off to ring a young eagle in an eyrie in Strathspey. We called at the keeper's house and he allowed us to take our Land-Rover across a bumpy hill track; then we had about three kilometres (2 miles) walking across rolling heather moorland to the eyrie, which was located in the cliffs above the river.

As we approached we had good views of the two parent eagles soaring over the hill near the eyrie. Suddenly a male merlin came chasing up towards them calling excitedly,

A newly fledged eaglet perches in an ancient Scots pine which provides a superb roost.

Eagle country in the Scottish Highlands.

'kick, kick, kick, kick, kick', and attacked them, despite the huge size of the eagles. The merlin rose above one of the eagles and then dived straight at it from about 15 metres (50 ft) above, almost passing through one of its wings. After a dozen or so dives and a lot more calling, the merlin drifted back across the moor towards its youngsters in their nest among the heather.

Two of us climbed along the far side of the river gorge but when we got to the eyrie we found that it was empty. There was all the evidence of recent occupation – remains of feathers and hare skins, lots of down and the obvious white droppings of a young eagle. We searched around and quickly found the eaglet standing in the heather about 45 metres (150 ft) along the cliff. We approached it, but it looked very fierce and made its first flight just before we could catch it.

When we finally caught it we ringed it and put it back into the eyrie, where-upon it immediately started to eat the remains of a hare carcase. We climbed back to the other side of the gorge and looked back to watch the eaglet eating. As we left, one of the adult birds glided about 100 metres above us and back over the hill behind the eyrie.

Since then my colleagues and I have ringed a large number of eagles. It gives us a chance to see eagles at close quarters, to discover more about their lives at the eyrie and to see what the parents have been feeding to their chicks. It is fascinating to work out the kinds of prey from tiny scraps of feather, fur or bone left in the nest. The chicks themselves can be very different in character. Some lie down quietly and it is possible to reach under the tail of the youngster, pull one leg gently out from underneath its body, put the ring on its leg and measure its wing without it rising or becoming agitated. On other occasions you look over the edge of the eyrie and the young eaglets are ready to fight anything that comes towards their nest. They stand upright, their wings spread in a threatening posture, their bills open; they sometimes call or hiss. As you get closer, they may strike with their talons. It is important never to hurt the birds and to hold them gently while carefully putting the rings on their legs. Yet, in a flash, a powerful needle-sharp talon can puncture your hand and draw blood, or the eaglets may catch your finger with their hooked bills.

People sometimes ask whether the eaglets are frightened, or seem to be stressed by the ringing procedure. They don't appear to be. After ringing them and gently placing them back in the nest, the birds immediately settle down. As you leave, their eyes follow you; they swivel their heads as you walk off, but once you get a sufficient distance away and look back, you see them walking about on the nest as though nothing had happened.

As the chicks prepare for flight, they are already as big as their parents, and as they perch on the nest they may even look bigger, for the much darker juvenile body plumage contrasts markedly with the paler golden feathers of the adult birds, which are often worn and faded at this time. The heads of the young are not as yet

A young eagle lumbering into flight.

*For the first few weeks after
learning to fly the eaglet stays
close to the nest area and is ever
watchful for the return of a
parent with food. This young
eagle was ringed in the nest
and the metal ring is just visible
among the feathers of the left leg.*

golden, more a rusty brown, and there is a very obvious yellow gape along the length of the bill. The cere is also bright yellow.

The parent birds no longer bring as much food to the nest, the growing period is over and the eaglets do not require as much as they did when half grown. Their wing feathers are almost complete and they will soon be ready to leave.

The last few weeks in the eyrie can be a pretty hectic time. In the week before they fly, it seems as though their legs are tethered to the nest by elastic bands as they bob up and down, eventually as much as 1 metre (3 ft) above the nest. In one nest, just behind some aspens and rowans on a cliff face, the youngsters sprang up and down, their huge wings touching the leafy foliage overhanging the nest. The bright green leaves and the white flowers of the trees, as well as the brilliant white wing patches and the white tail bands of the young eagles, all sparkled in the bright evening sun.

An inquisitive young eagle in its dark juvenile plumage.

At some eyries the eaglets can wander a little way from the nest along a ledge, or if trees are close at hand they may perch out on one of the branches. In raptors we call this 'branching' behaviour, a sign the young birds are leaving the nest and exploring their local environment. Sometimes a youngster will do more than just wander a few metres. One eagle pair which was filmed by the RSPB had a rather unusual nest in the heather beside a big rock. The eaglet left the nest on day fifty-five, well before it was able to fly, and slowly ambled up the hill over a period of a couple of weeks. Each day, or even for a few days at a time, it would settle down in the heather among the rocks and the parent birds would come and feed it. By the time it was ready to fly it had moved several hundred metres further up the hill, where it made its first flight at seventy-two days of age, seventeen days after it began its journey.

And what a day when the eaglet flies for the first time! It may not be much of a 'flight', just a short flutter along a cliff and a undignified crash-landing in the heather. Wildly beating wings, trying not to gain too much speed, flashing white patches against the dark brown plumage and the broadly spread white tail with a black band, a downward glide and a very hesitant landing. In nests with two young, when one has flown, the remaining sibling looks lost, peering out in vain.

After the first flight the young eagles often stay in their landing position for quite a long time, even for a day and a night, but the parent birds find them easily. The youngsters will yelp as soon as they see their parents, especially if they are carrying food. The parents will then come down and leave food for them where they have crash-landed. The chicks find it difficult to lift off out of the heather so they will scramble up on to a tree or rock, after struggling through the sometimes rank vegetation. They start to land with more control and grace and soon desist from landing in long heather. It is much easier to slip off the branch of a tree or an exposed rock for the next flight. On their sixth, seventh or eighth flight, they will probably make a return trip to the nest. Their younger sibling may still be there, and they know that this is the place to get food if they are hungry. The parent

After a few weeks of flight, even perching on one leg and scratching its bill with its huge talons is second nature to a young eagle.

birds still take food back to the nest at this stage, so it remains a focal point of the young eagle's life.

After two weeks of flying the young eagles are becoming proficient. Dry and breezy weather encourages them to fly and each day's outing gives them more strength and control. If there are two young they will fly together, playing 'tag'. One flies after the other and swoops down at it playfully, the other turns its wings and may even present its talons, or it may dive away. The two young eagles will go twisting through the sky together, testing their wings and becoming extremely proficient acrobats. This is important for the future.

Young eagles have slightly broader wings and longer tails than their parents and these confer advantages with regard to flying. They fly more slowly and gain more lift, and use smaller updraughts to keep aloft. The young eagle is better suited for soaring in search of carrion, which is its main food early in its independent life, before it acquires hunting skills.

Each evening, after a busy day's flying, the eaglets return to roost on the cliffs near to the nest site. The parent birds have favourite roosts quite close to their nesting eyrie and the youngsters soon learn where the best sites are located. If we could see them at night we would find the youngsters roosting quietly on a rock or a tree on the cliff face not far from their parents. By the end of August the young eagles will have followed their parents throughout the local parts of the home range.

Sometimes as you are walking in the hills in the late summer you will hear a squeaking eagle. If you look carefully you will see a youngster following its parent along the upper reaches of the crags above you. As summer gives way to autumn the young eagles may have made their first attempts at catching prey. These will have been unsuccessful, for much skill is needed to catch a rabbit or a grouse. Most of the time they are still relying on food caught by their parents, especially the male. This period of dependency on the parents can last two or three months and sometimes even further into the winter.

Detailed observations over several years at the golden eagle site in the Lake District, analysed by David Walker, showed that the young golden eagles stayed within the nesting valley for about six weeks after fledging and were supplied with fresh prey by the male. For a further two weeks they kept to the main hunting area of the male and were escorted by him. Only carrion was seen to be eaten after they left the valley. Eight weeks after fledging, they wandered further, still escorted by the male and were often seen in the outer parts of the home range. At about ten weeks the male rejoined the female and the juveniles wandered alone. They first left the home range at this stage and were judged to be fully independent when the adults used territory displays towards them at about eleven weeks. They were seen in the nesting valley for up to seventeen weeks after fledging and at least one wintered at the edge of the home range. It appears the female has little to do with provisioning the fledged young with food, most of the onus being placed on the male.

Drifting off at dusk to find a secure roosting place. Eagles use different roosting sites depending on weather and wind direction; it is most important to remember dry sheltered sites when rain storms blow in from the west.

Autumn Days

Red deer stags roaring in the hills and the grey geese from the Arctic calling as they pass over the mountains are the two sounds I associate with this season in the Scottish Highlands. The purple bloom of August has gone from the heather hills and they have a brown cast, the grasses and sedges withered, dry and tawny. The hill is bathed in yellowy golden light. In places, the birch trees have turned orange and red, while the rowans in their autumn colours are laden with bright, waxy red berries, a feast for the fieldfares and redwings from Scandinavia. High in the crags beside the old eagle nest the leaves of the aspen trees are the most brilliant yellow, in marked contrast to the cold grey of the rock face. Although some young eagles are still at home with their parents, others have left to start out on their own journeys in life.

Elsewhere in the northern world the autumn colours are also upon us, and eagles are restlessly preparing for the coming winter.

Mongolia. 19 September 1990. My three companions are ahead of me in single file on their Mongolian ponies. With two local guides, we have been riding north for three days along the Bulgan Gol, in the western mountains, camping each night beside the river. At this place the track is just a few metres wide beside the clear, cold, fast-flowing river. Above us, sheer cliffs of pale grey rock soar upwards for some 100 metres (300 ft), and way above there are snow-capped mountains. Vultures, lammergeiers, eagles and ravens have tracked our progress and now, as we turn our horses to ford the river, three adult golden eagles speed down the cliffs. Two males are displaying madly at a larger female. The extra male may be a visitor from further north or, more likely, the neighbouring male straying up river. They turn and start to sky dance in the bright blue sky and disappear behind a big jutting buttress overlooking the Bulgan Gol.

I stop my horse to admire three aspen trees growing by the river, their grey trunks casting shadows across the pebbly grey rocks where the river has flooded in its springtime torrents. The foliage is a brilliant golden yellow, absolutely flaming in the autumn sun; some of the outermost branches are black and skeletal, where the winds have blown away the first of the autumnal leaves. In a few weeks none of these beautiful leaves will remain and the scene will be cold and wintry.

Autumn is an easier time for eagles in the Scottish hills, especially where hunters are shooting red deer throughout the moors and mountains. Traditionally, after making a kill the stomach contents of the dead animal, called the gralloch, are left on the hill for the scavengers to eat. Golden eagles are quick to come down to the grallochs, along with ravens and crows.

Autumn is time for the adults to rest after rearing their young, although the young still follow them on hunting trips into the mountains.

Autumn time in the Scottish Highlands. The red stags start their annual rut and the hills resound with their roaring.

By this time the young eagles will probably have met eagles from other territories, and will soar with them in the sky. I often think that eaglets which grow up in a nest of two chicks have a much more exciting time after they leave the eyrie than the single chicks. Rob and Beryl Henderson wrote to me about two such youngsters which we had ringed in June 1986.

Easter Ross. 20 October 1986. We were exceptionally fortunate in having both young in sight for over four hours. At 11.10 a.m., both were seen flying together and landing in short heather on the skyline on the northern ridge. They were playing and jumping up at each other for a few minutes, then bird A [referring to the wing-tags with which I had marked the young] drifted off, while B remained stationary for over two hours on the hillside. Eventually it sailed off 800 metres (half a mile) to the cliff top above the eyrie used last year and remained perching there for a further eighty minutes. At no time was food brought in, nor the adults seen. Meanwhile, chick A was heard cheeping on the south side below the 1982 nest, and from time to time was seen quartering the cliff face among the autumn birches.

We know that most young eagles in Scotland do not move very far from where they were hatched; 160 kilometres (100 miles) away from its natal site would be a long journey for a Scottish eagle. The youngsters tend to come out of the mountains on to the lower moors and hills, avoiding the home ranges of adult pairs of eagles. Some of the places they live in through the autumn are places where eagles used to breed, but no longer do so because of interference or disturbance.

During the time that we wing-tagged eagles in the north Inverness glens, individual young eagles were sighted in the first winter to the south-east of where they were ringed. The colour tags are visible from 1 kilometre (0.6 miles) or so with good binoculars or a telescope. One young bird travelled down to the heather hills in Morayshire, where it spent the whole winter. Another was seen near Newtonmore, not far from the A9 road running between Perth and Inverness.

Young birds tend to wander to places where no adult eagles chivvy them, and in consequence they are quite often on poorer quality land or in dangerous or disturbed places. In October or November they have to find an area where they can make their home for the winter. Though there is plenty of food early in the autumn, as the nights of winter lengthen, the living becomes more difficult. They really need to be ready for the long cold winter ahead; need to learn where to roost, and to find the best trees for roosting in different kinds of weather.

They must also locate the best hunting grounds in their new area. Are there any rabbit warrens? How can they approach the rabbits without being seen from a long way away? Is there a chance of snatching one quickly from behind a particular rock? Where are the red grouse living, are there ptarmigan on the high hills, where are the mountains hares, and what other birds and animals live in this winter territory?

Eagles learn from a very early age that it is always worth finding out what

The eagle plucks a mountain hare before it eats it.

hooded crows and ravens are up to. They will often find a dead creature on the hill long before an eagle. So where young eagles search for their own food they also keep one eye on the other scavengers. As soon as the eagle arrives, the other birds will usually retreat and allow it to eat. Eagles also learn to put up with a lot of mobbing from other birds, especially ravens. They will come tumbling out of the sky, maybe three or four of them at once, and give an eagle a real buffeting, coming close enough to try to hold on to its tail feathers or the tips of its wing. A young eagle soon learns that there is no actual danger, just the nuisance of being pestered by these big, bold black birds. However, it may still turn suddenly, flicking over to smack the raven with its talons. Hooded crows also chivvy eagles mercilessly, giving away the presence of an eagle to other creatures by the noise that they make. When an eagle perches on a rock, bold and cheeky hooded crows will come very close: one in front of the eagle while others sneak up behind and pull its tail feathers. If they are too persistent the eagle may fly away and find a quieter place.

In the coldest areas of the northern world, golden eagles will migrate long distances in autumn to avoid the shortage of food created by deep, lasting snow and short hours of daylight. In the interior regions of North America and northern Europe and Asia, north of sixty degrees latitude, many eagles migrate south for the winter. In Europe, golden eagles ringed in Finland have been found as far away as Hungary and Ukrainskaya, at distances of over 2000 kilometres (1240 miles) and 1500 kilometres (930 miles) respectively. A few golden eagles appear at the traditional raptor migration sites such as Falsterbö, Sweden and the Bosphorus, Turkey. Most settle in areas already occupied by eagles, which makes it difficult to know if a bird is a migrant or a resident.

Montana. 23 October 1981. I have walked up from the ranger station at the top of Lost Horse Creek in the Bitterroot Wilderness and am standing on the State Line between Idaho and Montana. Bear Lake is just over 3 kilometres (2 miles) away and Fish Lake just over 6 kilometres (4 miles). Bruce, one of the rangers, is heading off into the wilderness for a two-day hike to check on various stations on the way.

Now alone, I turn north to follow the ridge and look across the mountains towards Missoula and down to the Bitterroot valley. It is cold up here at over 1830 metres (6000 ft) but there is no wind as such today, just very high white cloud with the palest of blue skies poking through in places; the air is crystal clear and cold. I am looking northwards along the ridge to row after row of jagged mountains. Even at this height there is a scattered tree cover of sub-alpine firs, Ingleman spruces and larches turning tawny orange. Here and there dead snags of trees are encrusted in yellowish-green lichens. A pair of mountain chickadees poke their black and white heads out of the thick pale green foliage to look at me and to squeak noisily at my passage.

In another tree a grey squirrel scolded me, though possibly he had also seen the male goshawk which shot over the ridge. A pair of ravens is cronking away to the north, and twenty-five pine grosbeaks have just flown by on migration. A couple of red crossbills shot by, followed by three brightly coloured cedar waxwings. The birds know the snow is coming and it's a day to migrate south. Another small group of three mountain chickadees call at me, and coming down the ridge from the north are six American robins clucking away; they are large thrushes with chestnut red plumage.

The evening light catches the young eagle at its roost and also the tiny bits of scattered white down preened from its plumage.

At last, at 12.50 p.m., I am at a pinnacle on top of the ridge and I can see an adult golden eagle soaring to the south, whirling around a rock summit about 1.6 kilometres (1 mile) away from me, with two ravens calling in attendance. A little later, as I start to descend towards a clear greeny-blue lake, a pair of golden eagles comes soaring down from the other direction. I am only a transient visitor to these beautiful wild peaks of the Bitterroots, so I am not sure whether these adult eagles belong here, or whether they are birds passing by from further north to winter on the broad plains to the south.

Looking down a gully full of old snow, peppered with the lightest covering of fresh snow from last night, I peer through a screen of autumn-tinted larches towards the bluest of lakes nestling below me. A bull elk is trumpeting in the distance among tall columns of dark spruces, merging on the other side of the lake into a thick dark forest.

Two days later friends loan me a four-wheel drive and I travel north out of Missoula towards Flat Head Lake. By midday I am in the bison reserve. I've seen American kestrels and red-tailed hawks. All the grassland has turned yellow; the flower heads are hard and dark against the yellow-tawny stems. The vegetation is nearly knee-high and, about 140 metres (450 ft) from the track, five prong-horned antelopes are grazing through long grass, their pale rumps obvious in the autumn sunlight. Further away across the plain, twenty-one bison are grazing at the bottom of the slope of a rounded hill. They are huge animals, even at this distance, and within this protected area one can get a feeling of what the great plains of America were like when bisons roamed them from end to end. Two golden eagles drift across the hill and perch in the crossbars of an electricity pylon at the edge of the reserve. This is real eagle country, with great places to hunt and broad horizons in which to see their prey; this is wild Montana at its best, the state they call the 'big sky'.

Back in Scotland in October, the geese have arrived from the Arctic. The pink-footed geese come down in late September and early October, flying high over the mountains in large skeins of a hundred or more birds, often at high speed. More interesting for eagles is the arrival of the greylag geese in mid October, some of them still coming through until mid November. These geese often travel in smaller parties and the weather can force them to fly low through the glens. Sometimes eagles will attack them as they pass. The old birds will sail out from their rocky lookouts and chivvy the passing skeins, while the geese set up a tremendous gaggle of calling and try to get out of the eagles' territory as quickly as possible. Sometimes a young goose will make a mistake and get separated from the flock. This is what the eagles are hoping for, because it is the younger, inexperienced birds they have a chance to fly down and kill.

In November the first real snows come to Scotland and the young eagles get their first taste of a Highland winter. Most of them will survive, for there is still an adequate food supply. The stalkers are culling red deer hinds and there will be plenty of grallochs in the heather or on the bloodstained snow to provide easy pickings.

The most dangerous part of any eagle's life is its first winter, for it is then that those birds which are failing to find enough food or secure safe roosts are likely to die. It is believed that only one out of every four fledged eagles actually survives to breed. The situation is probably worse than that because of the high levels of human persecution of eagles in many countries. Recoveries of ringed eaglets help us

An adult eagle cleans its bill after eating its prey – even the smallest piece of skin or blood is carefully removed during preening.

to understand mortality, but when birds are illegally killed this evidence is suppressed. The level of mortality suggests that it will take at least ten years for a pair of eagles to produce enough young to replace themselves.

The lifespan of eagles is another difficult question. An eaglet ringed in France was found dead at twenty-five years and eight months, while captive birds have lived to double this age. Several people have been certain that pairs of eagles they studied in the wild had been together for over ten years. I was certain that a pair I visited regularly over a similar period was the same and I do not know how old they were when I first got to know them. It is certainly possible that some eagles nesting in Scotland are well over thirty, but the age of the oldest is unknown. Ringing recoveries in Scotland have not yet given enough information, and the rings we used on eagles in the past were occasionally removed by the birds themselves.

When an old breeding eagle dies it is a major event for those others waiting to breed. If it is a female, young females compete to take over her territory and the old male. Sometimes the young female may not lay eggs in her first year, but soon she will breed. She learns from her mate the best places to hunt and the best places to roost. She visits the traditional eyries and, although she may choose roosting sites not used by the previous female, she learns many things from the male about that home range. Their life together may last ten years or more. Eventually the older male will die, and younger males will fight to take his place. The female chooses a male and he in turn learns from her some of the special characteristics of that particular home range. He will add his own idiosyncrasies, but in general he will maintain the long-held traditions of that home range.

In this way home ranges are passed from one generation to the next. Some are known to have been used for centuries, and it is likely that some sites have been used for thousands of years. It is very unusual for both adult birds to die at the same time, so the traditions of ages are handed down in a leap-frogging action between the sexes. This will only be broken during periods of intense persecution when both adults are killed and ancestral links lost.

While our eagles in Scotland are still months away from egg laying, and the northern lights are flickering away through the bitter cold nights of January, the most southerly golden eagles in North Africa and southern Europe have already started a new nesting season. They live in hot, arid places quite different from those I know at home. It is a quite different landscape but the bird itself is the same.

Corsica. 10 September 1982. The interior of the island of Corsica in the Mediterranean Sea has the most fantastic habitats for golden eagles. Standing on the roadside among the great spreading chestnut trees, their ripening fruit green inside their bundles, I look up into a clear pale blue sky to the most incredible pinkish rugged mountains, towering 1000 metres above me. In places there are dark vegetated ledges but mostly these are buttresses of pink granite. Pine trees grow high up on the ledges and in the lower areas there is a thick impenetrable jungle of head-high scrub, its aromatic scent heavy in the warm air.

High in the cliffs a pair of golden eagles has its eyrie. A straggling road etches across a heavily wooded rocky ridge running down into the valley, leading to the tiny red-roofed white houses of a village on the southern slopes of the next mountain.

Adult eagles regularly moult their feathers through the summer on a two-year cycle – one such body feather falls down among the heather blooms below the preening perch.

Some Problems for Eagles

There are many reasons for the decline of eagle populations throughout the world but the major one is man's influence on the environment, in addition to direct persecution and deliberate killing. In the British Isles, golden eagles are largely restricted to Scotland, mainly in the Highlands and Islands, with only a handful of pairs in south-west Scotland and northern England.

Though man has always admired the strength and majesty of the eagle, it has been mercilessly slaughtered. Fortunately, golden eagles never became extinct in Britain, and in recent decades, with changing attitudes towards wildlife and stricter wildlife laws, they have fared better. Yet every spring there are instances of people disturbing and harming golden eagles, despite the fact that they are a protected bird with a penalty of £5000 for killing or taking one.

When I was a child, egg collecting was practised by many small boys who had primitive collections gathered from the nests of blackbirds, thrushes and other common garden birds. Nowadays egg collecting is no longer acceptable and the stealing of rare birds' eggs is a serious offence. Eagles' eggs are, of course, most highly prized. Collecting, possession, and the challenge of finding the nest, evading detection by landowners, gamekeepers, wildlife wardens, the RSPB and the police, give the thieves their satisfaction.

After a long trek, a climb up through the leggy heather and a swing along through the birch trees, you peer over the rocks and look down into an empty nest. You had expected to see an eagle incubating or a couple of young chicks, but there is evidence that someone has been there before you and robbed the nest. The discovery of such destruction is distressing.

The theft of eagles' eggs in the Scottish Highlands is a well-planned operation. The thieves will be poring over maps during the winter, carrying out trial runs to test the best ways in and out of the glen and where to hide the getaway car, which often gives the game away. The thieves must act early in the season, soon after the birds have laid. Then the eggs are still in mint condition, for as the eagle sits the eggs become faded and marked. The egg shells also become thinner and more fragile and more difficult to 'blow' with a large embryo growing inside the egg.

During the twenty-five years I worked for the RSPB, we received telephone calls every spring from landowners, shepherds and gamekeepers about suspicious cars and people in places which suggested they were attempting to rob eagles'

Golden eagles are beautiful birds – superb symbols of wild places. But not everyone reveres them: too many are still killed or poisoned despite being specially protected by law.

Drying out after the rain.

nests. It was often difficult to prevent them carrying out their egg-thieving activities, but increasing numbers were apprehended as the RSPB's intelligence network got better and better. By the late 1970s, an egg thief coming to Scotland for eagle eggs stood a very good chance of being caught. The police of the Northern Constabulary have become extremely adept at detecting these wildlife crimes and successfully bringing the criminals to court. The courts have also realised that these crimes are more than boyhood pranks and are committed by people who know the illegality of their actions and are determined to circumvent the law.

Successful prosecution of egg thieves is based on a great deal of field knowledge, successful hunches, a lot of luck and long hours spent in the field. It seemed at times in March and April that there was no time to stop. Each group of thieves had only a few days in the Highlands to carry out their actions, whereas we were there full time and had to respond to each new threat as it appeared on the horizon.

With raptors, such as peregrine falcons and eagles, a new band of thieves has taken over from the egg collectors. In the 1950s any qualified falconer could take a young eagle from the wild and train it for hunting hares and rabbits. After the 1967 Bird Protection Act these activities were more strictly controlled under licence. It was illegal to take a youngster from the wild without the permission of the Nature Conservancy. But in the 1970s the demand for young eagles far outstripped the number that could be taken legally from the wild. The licensing system was based on a quota of five or six eaglets to be taken from the Scottish Highlands each year. Unfortunately, people realised that if the supply could not be met legally from the wild, there was money to be made by taking birds illegally.

Every year we would hear about eaglets that had disappeared from their nests, and we were convinced that birds were being taken to supply a trade in England, and probably the continent, especially in Germany. It was rare for us to catch any of these people, who were often in collusion with a local person working on the estate who wanted to get rid of the eagles. Over the years, however, we did have some success.

Inverness-shire. July 1977. We discovered that a falconer had a young eagle which he claimed to have bred in captivity. We were convinced that this was not the case and that the youngster had been taken from a nest, probably soon after hatching. Though we thought we had good information, the police were unable to take the case further because of legal difficulties. Some time later the police contacted me about this same eagle, now fully grown. The falconer was in custody in Inverness on another matter, and would I please come and take the eagle away.

Collecting the eagle was quite a problem. It was a very big bird indeed and we had a struggle getting it into the car. As I drove off, two falconer friends of the accused

It is surprising to many people that eagles are quite at home on the ground – sometimes they even hunt for frogs in wet grass and marshy places.

The eagle plucks its prey,
a brown hare.

man tried to prevent me leaving and attempted to take the eagle. The police had to escort me off the premises.

We kept the bird at my home but it was unfortunately already seriously imprinted by man. It would 'talk' to you with a querulous cheep, look at you and eagerly wait for you to come out and feed it. It was just like a family pet; obviously it had been looked after from the time that it was very small. We kept it for a short time on the lawn outside the house, where it encountered our young dog. The puppy ran out of the back door one day and straight towards the eagle. Without a second glance the eagle jumped on the dog and held her across its body. There was tremendous yelping, and my wife ran out and managed to beat the eagle off with a broom.

The poor puppy was in a terrible state, wheezing, with puncture marks in the side of her body. You could see the bubbles coming through the side of her body cavity. My wife hurried her in to the vet. It's not often you ask a vet to look at your dog because a golden eagle has caught it. Within a day or two, the puppy was back to her normal health and from then on she kept a wary eye on the eagle.

This eagle was a real character. It would perch on its block outside our house and as you walked out it would call at you. It really enjoyed human company and if you sat down it would stare at you with its big eyes, turning its head upside down to view you from a different direction.

We were given permission by the police to release the eagle and tried to rehabilitate it by keeping it with the young sea eagles ready to be released on the island of Rum. It stayed there for a few weeks before being released. But then it flew to the nearby island of Canna and became a nuisance – attacking ducks in a garden and following children going to school!

The poor bird had to be recaptured as it seemed to have lost all fear of humans, and would be a danger both to itself and to people if left in the wild. From then on it stayed in captivity, though even then, when it was trained for falconry, I heard that on one occasion it dived down and attacked a boy who was wearing an anorak with a rabbit-fur hood.

Another illegal trade in eagles involves the killing of adult birds for taxidermy. This was very difficult to track down as it could be linked with other, legal, trade between game dealers and hunters. We were pretty sure that people involved in trading red deer carcases to the continent were also supplying dead golden eagles for taxidermists. In the late 1970s a well-prepared golden eagle skin could fetch between £500 and £1000. Now the trade in taxidermy is licensed and any dead eagle must be shown to have died of natural causes. So eagles which are electrocuted on overhead power lines can be prepared as taxidermy specimens, but birds full of poison or lead shot are illegal specimens. The government has an inspection scheme to monitor these regulations.

Trapping, shooting and poisoning were widespread in Victorian times, and golden eagles became rare in many areas; other birds such as the sea eagle, the osprey and the red kite became extinct. It seemed that man thought that any predator which might damage his game or sport was not to be tolerated. Human persecution of eagles today is not as bad as it was in the early 1970s and 1980s, however, when persecution reached a post-war peak after relatively safe times for

Ptarmigan are found on the higher mountains in Scotland and are hunted by eagles. In winter, their white plumage gives them camouflage against the snow while in summer the plumage is grey brown. This bird is in transitional state.

eagles in the 1960s. Antagonism towards them is due to suspected predation on sheep or red grouse. On many occasions eagles are blamed for lamb deaths which are really due to bad weather, disease, poor condition or poor animal husbandry. Though eagles do occasionally kill lambs, it is easy to distinguish these from carrion by the bruising around the talon marks. Eagles may be more likely to take live lambs where the range on which the sheep and the eagles live has been badly damaged by overgrazing and burning.

When I first wandered the hills and glens in the early 1960s, the killing of birds of prey was regarded as routine and no one was particularly ashamed of doing it. Fortunately there were some landowners and keepers who were extremely proud of their eagles and would never harm them, but others were either unpleasant or indifferent. Pole traps were set in many places. A fence post driven into the open moor held a spring-jawed trap, and was the only place for a bird of prey to perch. When I first found these in action, I was horrified. I remember walking across a moor and finding a kestrel in one trap, a short-eared owl in another and a cuckoo in a third. I remember vividly finding a kestrel dead in one such trap. The little ring of bare earth around the bottom of the trap showed where the bird had struggled, day after day, flapping, with its foot in the trap, before finally dying of starvation.

Recently there have been cases of people catching golden eagles in gin traps. One of my colleagues was walking up a glen and found a gin trap which had been set on a branch of a low birch tree. It had done its work, for it was now on the ground and in it was a golden eagle. The eagle was still alive and my colleague retrieved it. When we took the bird to the vet, we found that three of the toes on the right leg had been severed by the trap and had to be removed.

We nursed the bird back to health and released it, feeling it was better off in the wild than in captivity, but I wonder how it managed to survive with only one toe on its right foot. As an adult bird, it knew how to hunt and how to find carrion, but it was unlikely to be as successful as an eagle with a full set of talons. The man who set the trap appeared in court and was fined several hundred pounds.

The shooting of eagles has been practised for many years. In Victorian times eagle eyries and roosting sites were known by the keepers on the estates. They would make a hide of stones in the scree below the nest, at the perfect range for gun or rifle, and cover the top with grass and heather. The youngest of the keepering staff would be sent there to sit and wait for the eagle to come back in the evening to its roost. As it did so the nose of the gun or rifle would poke through a slot in the roof of the hide – and another eagle would fall dead.

Even nowadays some of those ancient hides are visible in the rocks and boulder fields underneath nest sites, and it is particularly encouraging to see an eagle reclaim one of these nests, perhaps after an absence of more than a hundred years.

On rare occasions eaglets have been stolen from their eyries in Scotland for falconry purposes despite the possibility of massive fines for this illegal activity; on one occasion the stolen eaglet was retrieved by the police and successfully returned to its parents in the wild.

Most present-day owners and managers are proud of the presence of eagles. But only five years ago I was told by a visitor that there was a dead eagle lying below a cliff in Wester Ross. Two colleagues and I went to the place and found the eagle. On the nest we could see one dead chick and the dead female below was peppered with shotgun pellets. The only encouraging thing was that the other eaglet was still alive in the eyrie, and the male bird managed to feed and rear the eaglet on his own. The local police, despite intensive efforts, were unable to prove who had killed the bird.

Persecution of eagles takes place in most countries where they occur. Poison causes many deaths and in the United States eagles have even been shot and killed from light aircraft. Cash bounties were paid by eagle and coyote clubs, whose members were mainly Texan sheep farmers, and some pilots killed as many as 200 eagles a year. In 1945, one man claimed to have shot 1005 eagles; in 1946 another 867, and by 1952 a total of 8300. This appalling slaughter was banned in 1962.

The most disturbing way of killing eagles was by poison, used sometimes in the past, but with the advent of new agricultural chemicals with legitimate uses in the late 1960s, people who did not like eagles changed their methods of killing. The insecticides or rodenticides could be used in a concentrated form and injected into a dead rabbit or the remains of a fox or a deer. It was deadly against carrion eaters such as golden eagles, ravens and foxes, and completely illegal. Over the years we collected many carcases found poisoned on the hills. A hillwalker would phone the RSPB office and say that he or she was walking in a particular glen and had come across the remains of a dead deer and beside it were the carcases of two eagles. Whenever these cases occurred we investigated them and gave the evidence to the government laboratories and the police.

Some people would claim that, as there were always eagles on their land, the killings were having no effect on the eagle population as a whole. But what was happening was that as soon as the breeding pair was killed other young adults would try to move in and claim the unoccupied nesting territory. The two immature eagles would then be killed and another two youngsters would arrive, then another two, and so on. The publicity associated with killing golden eagles grew more heated during the 1970s and 1980s. Today the general public is appalled by the deliberate killing of eagles, and if someone finds a dead eagle they will report it.

During the 1982 eagle survey, we found the vast majority of sites subject to severe persecution were in the eastern part of the eagle range, mainly in Caithness, east Sutherland, Speyside, Deeside and Perthshire. In each case this coincided with areas managed principally for red grouse. There were isolated incidents only of severe persecution in sheep-farming areas on the western seaboard. The deliberate killing of eagles is still a problem and needs to be continually addressed.

Eagles have every right to live in their wild and beautiful places. The presence of eagles on a landowner's estate should be part of a contribution to the environment. If a landowner is caught killing eagles, or encouraging or allowing his staff to do so, he should not receive government funding in the form of agricultural or forestry support. Further means must be found to eliminate this persecution.

Eagles have roosted in ancient Scots pines for thousands of years and the ancient native forest is an excellent habitat for them. They do not fare well in dense commercial plantations of conifers.

Eagle Conservation

I have tried to convey my sense of respect for this magnificent bird. It is the icon of Scotland's wild hill country, and yet abroad it also adds to the special nature of its haunts. The future is bright, yet as I write there are renewed calls for the licensed culling of birds of prey where they are alleged to have a detrimental impact on red grouse stocks. Clearly, we need to maintain the conservation and research effort, not least in order to understand the changing fortunes of golden eagles.

In the 1960s the Scottish breeding population was thought to be about 200 – 300 pairs. Yet it was not until 1982, when the RSPB and the Nature Conservancy Council carried out a complete census, with significant help from eagle enthusiasts in the Scottish raptor study groups, that a more accurate estimate was available. The weather in 1982 favoured the survey and by the end of the season nearly every suitable eagle area in Scotland and England had been checked, with the remainder completed in 1983. It was hard work, and long hours were spent in the field, sometimes in atrocious weather and over very difficult terrain. We found 424 pairs of golden eagles occupying home ranges, with another 87 nesting areas occupied by single birds. A further 80-odd areas with historical evidence of breeding eagles were now empty. The tally was considerably higher than earlier estimates of the population, and we believed it was due to better survey techniques, although a genuine expansion in range also seemed to have occurred.

In 1982 there was evidence of less persecution than in earlier decades, with some long-deserted sites being reoccupied. The highest occupancy of ranges was in the western Highlands, whereas only half of the known sites were occupied in the eastern grouse moor areas of Grampian and Tayside, reflecting continuing persecution. Indeed, research by Adam Watson and colleagues has shown that in Deeside, in the eastern Cairngorms, numbers of pairs on grouse-moors decreased after 1946, and have remained low due to persecution. Yet on deer forest there, eagles are seldom persecuted and breed well.

Of the population as a whole, 45 per cent of the pairs on home ranges in spring successfully reared young. The highest success rate (63 per cent) occurred in the eastern Highlands where the food supply is better, whilst the lowest success (18 per cent) was in the northern moors of eastern Sutherland and Caithness. From the 260 nests in which eggs were known to have been laid, at least 189 (73 per cent) hatched successfully. Most of these pairs reared young, and by the end of the summer 182 pairs had produced at least 210 fledged young, giving a mean brood size for all successful nests of 1.11 young per nest.

A perched bird dries its plumage in the sun.

The broad plateau of the Cairngorms – fine eagle country.

The most productive pairs were in the eastern Highlands, with a mean of 1.26 young per breeding pair – about average for past years. The lowest mean brood size was 1.05 young in the Western Isles. The most important measurement of breeding success in large raptors is the number of young reared per total number of pairs occupying home ranges. The total production was 0.52 young reared per pair of eagles on home ranges. Again, the eastern Highlands had the highest production, with 0.8 young per pair, while the northern flows and moors recorded the lowest average production of 0.23 young. If the single pair which reared two young in Orkney (the site is now deserted) was discounted, the production in the north area fell to only 0.14 young per pair – a figure which may be too low to sustain the population.

A follow-up national survey was undertaken in 1992. The results suggest that the population is much the same as ten years earlier. There was a decrease in certain areas due, it seems, to less food (possibly linked with degradation of the home range due to heavy grazing by sheep and deer). In other areas there was an increase, especially in the south and east of the Highlands, where persecution seems to have lessened over the intervening ten years. And there have been some subtle changes. In the west Cairngorms, for instance, some of the ranges still occupied have birds using eyries deeper in the hills – away from parts now well frequented by people.

Sometimes the loss of eagles is not due to deliberate persecution by man but is the unexpected result of his activities. When I first watched eagles in the early 1960s, the Nature Conservancy Council was worried about the failure of eagle eggs to hatch, especially in the western Highlands, where the adult birds often fed on dead sheep. Eventually, this failure was linked to the amount of dieldrin sheep dip in the carcases of sheep which had died on the hill and had then been eaten by eagles. Dieldrin is a toxic chemical which was used as an agricultural insecticide during the 1960s. It was a very effective sheep dip for killing ticks, keds and other parasites. Like DDT, it had serious side effects. A voluntary ban was put on its use, which was later converted into a total ban, an unpopular move with shepherds, who often blamed it on the conservation bodies. However, it is perhaps significant that countries such as Australia and New Zealand had banned the same chemical because of its potential damage to our food.

Nowadays, addled eggs are still collected from eagles' nests and sent to government laboratories for analysis. The presence of dieldrin has all but disappeared. More recently, detectable amounts of polychlorinated biphenyls

Red deer numbers in Scotland
have been very high in recent
decades and in many areas the
home range of the eagles has been
over-grazed by too many deer and
sheep. This has led to decreases
in live prey, such as red grouse
and mountain hare. Although
eagles will eat deer carrion,
the loss of live prey will have
serious consequences for
successful breeding.

The future for golden eagles
is varied; better protection,
enlightened attitudes to wildlife
conservation and the regeneration
of the native forests, especially
in conservation areas, is offset
by illegal persecution and
range deterioration.

(PCBs) have been found in eagles feeding on seabirds. This chemical travels through the marine food chain, but present levels in eagles seem to cause no immediate concerns for these birds in Scotland. Some of these pollutants are detected from the feathers of eagles, and researchers are currently sampling skins from museums to compare old and contemporary levels.

The rays of the setting sun on Ben Nevis, Scotland's highest mountain.

My own view is that the most critical issue for golden eagles today is the long-term degradation of their upland environment, and subsequent loss of biological productivity. Too many sheep and deer have grazed on lands which were once a rich ecosystem of natural forest, scrub and pasture. After at least two centuries of sheep grazing and poor burning, the accumulated gains of thousands of years of natural forest and shrub have gone. Much of the land is impoverished and this is made worse by high rainfall, thin soils, steep terrain and underlying acidic rocks. The result is a widespread and continuing decline in hares, red grouse and a range of other wild animals and ground-nesting birds – all natural prey for eagles. At least two lines of evidence support this view. First, since the beginning of this century sporting estate bag records of red grouse have declined, most markedly in the western Highlands and Islands. Second, there have been substantial declines in the extent of heather on the hill: some 18 per cent disappeared between the mid 1940s and mid 1970s.

Many eagles have been reduced to feeding almost solely on carrion, possibly a reflection of environmental degradation. Research has shown that in the west the population of adult eagles is high, perhaps because the large amounts of carrion there sustain eagles over winter. But their breeding success is poor because there seems to be very little live prey for the healthy development and growth of chicks. In the eastern Highlands the adult population density is lower, possibly because of persecution and a lack of suitable nest sites. Yet they breed more successfully here because of the larger numbers of live prey such as mountain hares, ptarmigan and red grouse.

In the 1970s and 1980s, there were many large-scale afforestation programmes in the Highlands. The trees planted were almost exclusively non-native conifers from North America, and this kind of tree farming caused serious change to the land as well as to eagles and some of the other upland birds. Once more than 40 per cent of the eagle's hunting ground (below 450 metres (1500 ft)) has been planted with conifers, the food supply becomes too impoverished for them to rear their young. First they cease to breed successfully, and finally they give up.

Although an eagle's home range may be up to 4800 hectares (12000 acres) in size, consisting of mountain, moorland, glen and loch, they use some parts much more intensively than others. The RSPB is currently studying range use by eagles, to work out how eagles divide up their territories and which types of land are most important to them. Most of the eagle's hunting activity takes place over only 2000 hectares (5000 acres) or so of the range. They prefer the places where they can surprise prey and catch it. There are areas, too, which are chosen for hunting prey in particular weather conditions, or certain directions of wind. Out on the regular bounds of their home range there are places where they rarely hunt, but which are important borders with neighbouring pairs.

Internationally, the Scottish population of 424 pairs of golden eagles is very important and requires special protection and conservation. The population is generally healthy, human persecution has been reduced, and there is reasonable breeding success. But the real future for the golden eagle in Scotland, as elsewhere in the world, rests upon the state of the land.

Strathspey. 12 September 1994. The scattered pines are casting long shadows in the low light of evening. On the hills the purple bloom is starting to fade but closer to hand in the shelter of the old forest the heather is still bright purple. There's a constant buzzing of bees and a distinct smell of honey on the faint breeze. Ten minutes ago a young kestrel passed over the purple moraines in front of me, their slightly damper ridges becoming yellow as the grasses turn colour. A couple of crested tits indignantly purred from the wood, and four meadow pipits landed at the edge of the small loch where a mallard was swimming.

I've been looking across a half kilometre or so to the wood where the eagles nested this summer. I'd seen no movement at all until a few moments ago when one of the young eagles was disturbed briefly by three hooded crows. It changed perches and was quickly hidden again in the foliage. I expect the whole family is there, about to roost through another night.

They have probably had a pretty good day, for the weather has been sunny, with a breezy wind ideal for soaring, and excellent visibility for hunting grouse and hares. And now that the stalking season has started there will be grallochs left in the heather.

What new skills did the youngsters learn this week? They may now know that red grouse like to eat juicy red cowberries in autumn along the burnsides. They've probably started to appreciate that rifle fire means dead deer, fresh grallochs and a full crop. All this information is stored for future use. With such good parents in such a richly provided home range these two youngsters have a good expectation of a long life.

We must never take these birds for granted, for they are the beacons of our mountain country. But we now need a wiser approach to the management of the land, to embrace the health of the ecosystem and the sensitive development of farming, forestry, sport-related management, tourism and conservation. Then there will be a chance of a richer future, not only for golden eagles, but also for us.

'…Close to the sun in lonely lands,
Ringed with the azure world,
he stands.'
Alfred Lord Tennyson

94

PHOTOGRAPHING GOLDEN EAGLES

19 December 1992. I awoke just before 6 a.m. The previous evening I had only just managed to drive my camper van to the end of the track leading to the top of a remote west Highland glen before a heavy fall of snow in the night had made the road out of the glen barely passable. It was to be another four days before I had any further contact with another person, a shepherd who arrived one evening in his Land Rover to check if all was well.

I climbed up to the hide and despite the cold I was hot from carrying 18 kg (40 lb) of equipment the 300 m (1000 ft) up the mountain. I first had to locate and then clear the snow away from the carcass of the red deer stag that a friend and I had laboriously dragged up there the previous day. I had built the hide three months earlier from rocks against a massive boulder at the foot of a steep slope composed of loose scree, just the type of material I needed to construct my igloo-shaped shelter. I crawled in, lit a candle and began to unpack and set up my cameras, conscious that I needed to be prepared by first light when the eagles could be leaving their roost-site in a gully on the opposite side of the Glen. With the arrival of dawn a wind got up and began to blow drifting snow against the deer carcass outside.

Presently nine hooded crows flew in and were soon jostling for position on the stag. Satisfied that they were oblivious to my presence I began taking photographs of them. After a little while the scene was becoming distinctly hazy. Un-coupling the camera body from the lens, I discovered a layer of snow had gathered inside the lens hood and was piling up against the front surface of the glass itself, although it was almost a metre from the outer edge of the hide wall. To have withdrawn the lens for cleaning at this point would almost certainly have disturbed them and, in turn, possibly alerted any eagles flying overhead that something was amiss on the ground, so I re-mounted the camera on to the lens and just watched the crows. Suddenly, and for no apparent reason, they flew off. They had done a good job of clearing the snow off the carcass. I withdrew the lens, scooped out the snow and dried the glass as best I could with a corner of my shirt.

For a moment I paused and glanced up through the gap in the scrim netting which veiled the rock porthole in the hide wall. To my utter surprise, I saw the female eagle standing perfectly still on top of the carcass. I froze, hardly daring to blink in case I disturbed her. She seemed not to be looking at the hide but up to the ridge which rose above and behind it, possibly at the crows which she had displaced. Eventually she relaxed and shifted her attention to the carcass and began tearing at the hide to gain access to the flesh beneath. Without taking my eyes off her, I began the painstaking process of re-positioning the camera and replacing the veil of netting around the lens. In the fifteen minutes she stayed she had made a sizeable hole in the carcass and I had taken over 120 photographs of her. I saw no more of the eagle that day and when the crows did return they behaved nervously, constantly glancing up at the sky. I stayed in the hide until 5.30 p.m., when it was quite dark and there was no possibility of being seen. This was important because I needed to use the hide in the days that were to follow. After five days the rain came, thawing the snow sufficiently for me to drive out of the glen safely and get home in time for Christmas.

This was perhaps the most memorable of all the experiences I gained over the four years spent taking the pictures for this book. Memorable, because it was the first time I had managed to get reasonably close to an eagle outside the breeding season. Previously, most of my efforts had been concentrated on recording the birds at their eyrie in the gully on the opposite side of the glen. As with all photography of protected birds in their breeding season, this was only possible after first gaining a licence from the government body responsible for nature conservation in the region: Scottish Natural Heritage. In the UK, the principles for photographing birds at the nest have been developed over decades. Because of the limitations

of early camera technology, pioneering bird photographers were forced to exploit situations where they could get close to their subjects. Since birds are necessarily drawn to particular sites to breed, this explains how the principles of nest photography were established. Over the years this has led to practically all British bird species being photographed at the nest time and again, including golden eagles. It also seemed a good place for me to begin. Through spending long periods photographing and observing eagles at eyries with their young I also came to learn much about the habits and movements of the adults. For example, I found that by noting wind direction it became possible to predict the route a bird might take when returning to the eyrie. Usually, they would fly into the wind to make use of the up-draught. This proved very useful when attempting flight photography. The chicks helped alert me, too, by calling loudly whenever they spotted a returning adult, often from a great distance, although they were occasionally fooled by passing aeroplanes! In future seasons I went on to build other more permanent hides further away from the eyrie but overlooking known flight-paths leading to it. Many were built from rock to blend in with the landscape and, unlike a standard fabric hide, were more likely to withstand the severe gales often encountered at such heights, though not, as I was later to find, avalanches of snow which swept one away without trace. They all had waterproof sheeting incorporated into their roofs which was then covered with turfs secured with wire netting. Most were large enough to sleep in for times when I had to spend long periods on the mountainside. Whenever possible I would build these hides months in advance of when I planned to use them, and never visited them in between time so the eagles were less likely to associate them with people.

When working at the eyrie, a companion would climb up to the hide with me then leave, with instructions to return at a pre-arranged time, the thinking being that on seeing someone walking away from the site, the birds would think it safe to return since they are unable to count. Likewise, on my companion's return, they would not be alarmed by emergence from the hide. Inevitably, this traffic caused some disturbance, albeit temporary. For nesting eagles the bond between adults and young overcame this problem but I was never convinced that this technique would prove infallible when attempting to photograph eagles away from the eyrie, such as at favoured perches they would use around their territory. If they were the least bit suspicious they would not return and there were always plenty of alternative perches they could choose, so I would only enter and leave the hides under the cover of darkness. Even then, I had to be prepared to stay for however long it took before the bird appeared. For one particular photograph this amounted to over 170 hours spread over four sessions.

Finding my way up and down the mountains in the dead of night was never much of a problem, as by working the same sites time and again I became familiar with all the features in the landscape, including the sheep and deer trails which I used over many of my routes. In the course of the project I climbed over 61,000 m (200,000 ft), often carrying photographic equipment, hide materials and all the other paraphernalia such as sleeping bags, stoves, food, and water I would need simply to allow me to spend long periods waiting for the eagles to appear. Despite all of this, success could never be guaranteed. All too often I would witness interesting behaviour which would be tantalisingly out of reach of even the longest of my telephoto lenses. At other times bad weather, particularly in the form of rain and the associated low cloud and mist would hang over the hills, preventing any photography whatsoever. In between, I would have rare, but very special days where my luck would change and I would obtain valuable pictures, which are the ones I value most. Most precious of all, however, was the time I spent in the company of these magnificent birds.

LAURIE CAMPBELL